Daddy Won't Cry Anymore

One Man's Journey to the Truth

DADDY WON'T CRY ANYMORE

JOHN CARR

Belleville, Ontario, Canada

DADDY WON'T CRY ANYMORE
Copyright © 2021, John Carr

All Rights Reserved. No part of this publication may be reproduced, stored in a retrieval system or transmitted in any form or by any means—electronic, mechanical, photocopy, recording or any other—except for brief quotations in printed reviews, without the prior permission of the author.

All Scripture quotations are taken from *The Holy Bible, New International Version* ®. Copyright © 1973, 1978, 1984 by International Bible Society. Used by permission of Zondervan Publishing House. All rights reserved.

Cataloguing data available from Library and Archives Canada

ISBN: 978-1-4600-1333-5
E-book ISBN: 978-1-4600-1334-2
(E-book available from the Kindle Store, KOBO and the iBooks Store)

To order additional copies, visit:
www.essencebookstore.com

Guardian Books is an imprint of *Essence Publishing,* a Christian Book Publisher dedicated to furthering the work of Christ through the written word. For more information, contact:
20 Hanna Court, Belleville, Ontario, Canada K8P 5J2
Phone: 1-800-238-6376 • Fax: (613) 962-3055
Email: info@essence-publishing.com
Web site: www.essence-publishing.com

Dedication

To my Heavenly Father, who drew me to His Son Jesus Christ; the One who took my punishment so I could have eternal life.

To my precious wife, Karen, who is the embodiment of Proverbs 31—the wife of noble character and a gift from the hand of God.

To my wonderful children—Julianna, Patrick, Caitlin, and Emilie—the arrows who fill my quiver. I love you with an unending love.

To friends, family members, and other individuals who have been a support and encouragement to myself and my family.

And a special thank you to my daughter Caitlin, and my friend Jake Letkeman whose own writing inspired me to get my story on paper.

Every good and perfect gift is from above,
coming down from the Father of the heavenly lights,
who does not change like shifting shadows.
(JAMES 1:17)

Contents

Prologue 9

Growing Up 11

Spiritual Seeds (Part 1) 19

Spiritual Seeds (Part 2) 43

Spiritual Seeds (Part 3) 61

Lakeshore Pentecostal Camp 89

Searching 99

Epilogue 117

Resources 127

*He will cover you with his feathers,
and under his wings you will find refuge;
his faithfulness will be your shield and rampart.*
(PSALM 91:4)

Prologue

"For I know the plans I have for you," declares the Lord...
(JEREMIAH 29:11)

It was a mid-August evening in 1992 and my gut was in knots. I was frantic, and I needed answers—NOW! "Tim," I said anxiously, as he and Linda, friends who had come to our house for a Bible study that evening, were about to walk through my front door. "Can we go for a walk? I need to talk to you." Tim responded, "Sure." I quickly walked out the door with Tim and, without making eye contact with my family or Linda, said that we would be back in about half an hour in time for supper.

With my heart pounding at a pace a racehorse could only compete with, and my head swimming with unending, unanswered questions just waiting to jump out of my mouth, we set out on our walk. The direction we were walking was of little concern to me as I began grilling Tim with my questions. The more I asked, the more frustrated I became, especially at the calm disposition Tim displayed amid my fear, anxiousness, and uncertainty.

DADDY WON'T CRY ANYMORE

Being considerably late, Linda and my two-year-old daughter Emilie went for a drive to find us (unbeknownst to me)—we (at least myself) had lost all track of time. I was later told that Linda and Emilie had seen Tim and me walking up a hill toward their vehicle without us seeing them. Rather than interrupting us, they just watched us from the vehicle. Linda turned to Emilie and asked, "Do you think Tim will be a good friend for your daddy?" Emilie replied, "Yes, because now my daddy won't cry anymore."

From the mouth of babes, my two-year-old daughter spoke prophetic words that were about to come to life in ways I would never have imagined…

Growing Up

For You created my inmost being; You knit me together in my mother's womb.

(PSALM 139:13)

God did indeed knit me together in my mother's womb and I was born into this world, a whopping 6 lb. 14 oz. boy, on December 23, 1959, at the Oshawa General Hospital (in Oshawa, Ontario), into the hands and care of my loving parents, Dawn Jean Carr and John (Jack) William Carr. I was the third of four children with two older sisters—Kara (the oldest), Janice—and one younger sister, Nancy, who would be born four years later.

Our home was located north of the city of Oshawa, known as the home of GM (General Motors), in a small country subdivision called Kedron. The house we lived in was built by my father, a self-taught carpenter whose work would rival that of a licensed or papered journeyman. Yet, despite the many ways in which Dad was gifted, he was never boastful and never self-promoting; he was a quiet, soft-spoken man—traits that were also evident in his stepbrothers, my uncles.

From her first marriage, my grandmother, on Dad's side, had three sons—my uncles, George (who played for the Toronto Marlies—the Toronto Maple Leaf's farm team), Frank, and Carl (who was killed in WWII during the Dieppe Raid in 1942). Her first husband, as the story goes, was murdered on the shipping docks (possibly being in the wrong place at the wrong time) during the 1930s, somewhere in the States. There was some speculation that it was the result of a gangster hit, but to my knowledge, nothing was proven. Grandma later married John William Carr I (my grandfather), and they had my Dad, John William Carr II. Dad's father, my grandfather, died when Dad was thirteen years old; consequently, he was left to be raised by Grandma, who never remarried after that, looking to his stepbrothers as father figures.

On reflecting on my years growing up at home, I regret the many more things I could have learned from Dad if it were not for some of my mixed priorities during adolescence. Although not often, my relationship with Dad became testy, but as I grew older and into a young adult, our relationship became close. I remember during a visit one time, sitting in the basement of my parents' place watching Dad do some brickwork for the fireplace. We chatted as he worked, and as I watched him, the words, "I love you, Dad," came jumping out of my mouth. Dad suddenly stopped working, seemingly caught off guard, and turned to me and said, "I love you too, son." It was a special moment that greatly impacted me as I am sure it did him also. I greatly miss him since his passing on March 21, 2018.

While Dad was born in Toronto, Ontario, Mom was born in the motor city—Oshawa. Mom came from a family

Growing Up

of four children—two sisters (my aunts Janice and Judy) and a brother named Jerry, my uncle. Mom was the oldest of the four. Like many at the time, Mom grew up during the Depression as well as during WWII. Times were tough, but her Mom and Dad, my grandmother and grandfather, were able to scratch out a living together to look after their family. Though times were challenging, time was found for some recreation in the form of dancing. Mom used to go to a well-known dance hall called The Jubilee Pavilion located on the shore of Lake Ontario in Lakeview Park. It was here that Mom met Dad, which later led to their marriage in 1951. Years later, I remember Dad relaying the story of how one evening while dancing at The Jube, there were a large number of people on the dance floor, all at one time. Consequently, the antiquated floor collapsed! Fortunately, there were no injuries. Who thought that dancing could be hazardous to your health?

Mom was a loving individual, who cared for her family, was a tremendous homemaker, loved to laugh, had a strong backbone, spoke her mind, was creative, and was a disciplinarian if she needed to be. She also went back to school (during my teen years) to pursue training as a Registered Nursing Assistant (RNA). Consequently, Mom worked at a Detox Centre, in the Whitby Psychiatric Hospital, and was then hired by the Oshawa Clinic, where she worked until retirement. By this time, Mom and Dad had purchased a lakefront lot up in Ontario's northern bush, a stone's throw from Algonquin Provincial Park, where Dad built their retirement home. Mom was now free to join Dad up north, away from the busyness of the city.

Mom loved crafts and painting, and upon joining Dad up north, she was able to devote more time to these hobbies. I remember Dad designing and building a craft area in the house, solely dedicated to Mom where she could work and create. She was so proud of her little shop.

I remember many times, after I left home, calling Mom on the phone to talk. Dad could always tell when Mom was talking with me because she would be laughing so much. Mom had a great sense of humour, as did Dad, and I miss our conversations. Not only do I miss our conversations, as I do Dad's, but I also miss her since her passing on January 16, 2019.

Having worked within the education system as a classroom teacher, special education teacher, principal, and psychologist I had the opportunity to be witness to children and teenagers who came from very challenging and heart-wrenching situations. I was also privy to several family dysfunctions that negatively affected some of the young people I had the privilege to work with. Experiencing this made it crystal clear just how blessed I was to grow up in the family I was given. I had parents that loved and cared for me and my sisters, I had siblings that loved me, as I did them, and we lacked for nothing. We were encouraged to be a part of and involved with community sports and clubs, there was always food on the table, clothing on our backs, and security (emotional and physical). In addition to that, Mom and Dad genuinely enjoyed spending time with us.

There are many fond memories of things we did as a family as well as times when we did things with Mom and Dad, or with my siblings, on a one-on-one basis. There were many trips to the back meadow and woods, not far from our house, to catch meadowlarks in their

Growing Up

nests, minnows out of the creek, build forts with my cousin and sisters, or just hike the bush. Many times, my sister Janice and I would head to the back woods with our pet raccoons, Bonnie and Clyde, to go for a walk and catch minnows for them to eat.

The raccoons came to be part of our family through Dad. It was a well-known fact that Dad loved animals and, while at work one day, a fellow employee came to him and asked if he would be interested in adopting two young raccoons who had been orphaned recently. Dad, given his softness toward the critters, agreed and we became the proud owners of two baby wild animals (without Mom knowing at the time). They were, by no stretch, the talk and curiosity of our neighbourhood—and those critters were quite the characters! One of my siblings relayed the story of our neighbour Dick Moses who was out in his garden hoeing his crops. Behind him was a fence on which, unbeknownst to Mr. Moses, was perched one of our raccoons. Each time Mr. Moses straightened up after each stroke of the hoe, the raccoon would reach out and try to snatch the hat off his head. One time, Mr. Moses sensed something moving behind him and turned—it was quite a sight to see. The shock and surprise on his face, I was told, were priceless!

We grew very fond of these pets, as did Mom, but after a year, we felt it was time to release them back into the wild. So, we headed up north to my grandparents' cottage, loaded them into a cedar strip motorboat, and headed for the beach on the north end of Red Stone Lake. As we approached the shore, we unlatched their cage and then, once onshore, coaxed them out of the boat. It was an emotional experience, to say the least. We climbed back into

DADDY WON'T CRY ANYMORE

the boat, while at the same time preventing Bonnie and Clyde from jumping in with us, and pushed offshore. With some distance between us and our beloved raccoons, we watched with heavy hearts as they stood on a rise behind the beach looking at us and then at each other, after which they disappeared into the forest. We headed back to the cottage with a sense of emptiness, but reassurance we had done the right thing—I guess Dad's softness toward animals had rubbed off on his kids after all.

In addition to the raccoon experience, we had many other fun times as well. Things such as camping trips to the East Coast during summer holidays, trips to Grandma and Grandpa's cottage, fishing on Red Stone Lake and at Honey Harbour, working together at home on select projects, tabletop hockey games in the basement of our house, and, of course, watching "Hockey Night in Canada" with Dad and Mom as she ironed clothes. I can still smell the vinegar and water solution she would spray on the clothes as she worked on them at the ironing board. I fondly remember those nights when Dad and I would race downstairs (with a bag of salt and vinegar chips) when we heard the "Hockey Night in Canada" theme music, to take our seats in front of the television—me on the couch and Dad in his chair with his mug of Labatt's 50. Mom would soon follow with a platter of goodies (cheese, pickles, and crackers) and a pot of tea for all of us to enjoy while we cheered our beloved Maple Leafs; Mom, however, was a Habs (Montreal Canadians) fan which made for some lively discussion when both teams were playing. At one point Mom refused to watch when both teams were playing because she would get so emotionally worked up!

Growing Up

There was also the pellet gun range that Dad had set up in the basement of our house. We took turns shooting at a target located at one end of the basement while sitting or laying down with the pellet gun at the opposite end. The only rule was that if someone were coming downstairs, they would have to yell to warn us they were coming so they did not accidentally get shot! At times, we would have to duck due to pellets bouncing back at us after hitting the target, which was located in front of a brick wall—boy, things were different back then! There were also the duck hunting expeditions to Lake Scugog. Dad would rouse my sister Janice and me from our beds around 4:30 a.m. and while we were getting dressed, Dad would be at the kitchen stove warming up some Lipton's Cream of Mushroom soup to put in the thermos, as it was usually chilly on the lake during those fall mornings. Once we got to the lake and loaded the old cedar strip motorboat into the water, we headed to Dad's pre-planned ambush location to surprise his quarry. I was assigned the job of bailing the boat, as it leaked like a sieve. They were cold, early mornings, but memories I will always cherish.

The majority of my growing up years were wonderful, having opportunities and experiences that other kids my age only dreamed about, due to the fact Mom and Dad invested time in and with us—a fact that later influenced me as a parent. But we were not a perfect family. We also had our share of challenges and struggles at times, but I am thankful our family held together.

There were many other memorable activities and events that occurred at the Carr house over the years which could be recorded in a book all on its own, but one thing, as I look back on my life, is that even though I was not aware of it at the time, God was drawing me to Himself through spiritual seeds being planted or sown through my family and others while growing up in Kedron.

Spiritual Seeds (Part 1)

*"No one can come to me [Jesus]
unless the Father who sent me draws him..."*
(JOHN 6:44)

In Matthew 13, Mark 4, and Luke 8, the parable (a story to teach a spiritual truth) is told by Jesus, to the crowd that gathered around Him, about a farmer who went out to sow his seed. Jesus says, *As he was scattering the seed, some fell along the path, and the birds came and ate it up. Some fell on rocky places, where it did not have much soil. It sprang up quickly because the soil was shallow. But when the sun came up, the plants were scorched, and they withered because they had no root. Other seed fell among thorns, which grew up and choked the plants. Still, other seed fell on good soil, where it produced a crop—a hundred, sixty or thirty times what was sown* (Matthew 13:4-8).

He then goes on to explain the meaning of this parable to his enquiring disciples. Jesus says, *The seed is the word of God. Those along the path are the ones who hear, and then the devil comes and takes away the word from their hearts, so that they may not believe and be saved. Those on the rock are the ones who receive the word with joy when they hear it, but they have no root. They believe for a while, but in the time of testing they fall away. The seed that fell among thorns stands for those who hear, but as they go on their way they are choked by life's worries, riches and pleasures, and they do not mature. But the seed on good soil stands for those with a noble and good heart, who hear the word, retain it, and by persevering produce a crop* (Luke 8:11-15; Mark 4:15-20).

In looking back, I do not ever remember being cold toward God or the things of God. I remember always having a softness toward Him and church, but I did not understand, until later in life, what it meant to be a Christian and what it meant to have saving faith. I would have to say I fit well into Jesus' description of the seed along the path—the one who heard the Word of God, but then had it stolen from my heart by the enemy (Satan) so I would not truly believe. I also fit well into the description of the seed that fell among thorns—life became so busy and all-consuming, that I was distracted and unable to hear from or about God. Though I felt I was in right standing with Him, Scripture showed me my true condition—that I was not seeking after God, it was God who was seeking after me (John 6:44; 1 John 4:19). In my state, I stood condemned before God and under His wrath because of my sin, I was spiritually dead, I was far from God, I belonged to the kingdom of Satan and was under his control, and I was an enemy of God (Philippians 3:18-19; Romans 3:11; 5:10; John 3:18, 36; Acts 26:18; Colossians 2:13; Matthew 15:8; Proverbs 15:29).

It wasn't that I was as bad as I could be; or that I lived out my sinful behaviour to its fullest; that I was incapable of acts of kindness; that I didn't have a desire to do good, or show goodwill; that I couldn't appreciate goodness, beauty, honesty, decency, or excellence, but it DID mean that NONE of this gave me favour with God, nor did it have any merit with Him. Because of my sin, and how that sin polluted every area of my life—including my conduct—my best efforts and attempts at moral living were as filthy rags in God's sight (Isaiah 64:6). Even my attempts at external conformity to Biblical teaching did not undo the effect and control of sin in my life. I needed a Saviour who could rescue me from that sin. That Saviour had to come from outside of myself, namely, Jesus Christ (Colossians 1:13; John 14:6; Matthew 9:6; Ephesians 2:4-5; Romans 5:16), and God wanted to deal with and save me from my sin and its consequences, through Him (1 Timothy 2:4).

It was a long process of God preparing, cultivating, and softening the soil of my heart until my early thirties when I became like that good soil Jesus talked about—He never gave up pursuing me. I thought I was that good soil all along, up to my early thirties, but I eventually realized I was fooling myself and was blind. Though I was unaware, God had been planting seeds in and cultivating my heart all along, desiring to draw me to Himself, and those seeds began being sown when I was a young boy growing up at home.

As I mentioned earlier, I grew up in a loving home where my parents openly cared for us and were not hesitant in showing us affection, but I would not say we would admit to being a religious family, although we would identify as being Christian—at the very least, Catholic.

Dad was the primary influence in my life at home and, whether or not he realized it, was an instrument used by God to sow spiritual seeds in my life. It was he that would encourage us and bring us to church—St. Gregory Catholic Church—each Sunday during our younger years (Dad was raised with a Catholic background). I clearly remember our Sunday morning routine. Mom would help to get us up and ready to go and then we would climb into the station wagon and head to town. After church, Dad would take us to Mr. Donut (a favourite stop-off for Dad) where we would enjoy some scrumptious donuts—my favorite was a French Crueller and my Dad's was an Apple Fritter—and sip on some coffee. After the donut stop, we would head to the Oshawa Airport where we would sit and watch the planes take off and land—I remember the tail section of a Lancaster Bomber from WWII was parked in the grass by the main building. Dad had such a love for aircraft and flying, as he was in Air Cadets when younger (during the latter part of WWII), and almost completed getting his pilot's license as a young adult.

As we got older, our trips to church grew sporadic, and usually, when we did go, it was only on the "important days" (e.g., Christmas and Easter). Even though going to church regularly eventually stopped, I remember observing how Dad displayed respect for God, how he demonstrated gentleness, and how he was diplomatic and polite with others. Do not get me wrong, Dad was not perfect and had weaknesses and failures like you and me, but in the midst of that, I could see that Dad had a form of reverence for things of faith. I remember wandering into my Mom and Dad's bedroom one day to look at Dad's exhaustive collection of *National Geographic* magazines (he collected them for thirty years!) that he had neatly stowed on the lower shelf of his nightstand. I remember using

Spiritual Seeds (Part 1)

some of them in my classroom, when I became a teacher many years later, as they contained some very interesting articles that my students benefitted from.

While perusing the magazines, my eye caught the spine of a smaller black book nestled to the side of the magazines. Upon closer examination, I realized it was a copy of the Holy Bible. It was the first copy I had ever seen in our home, yet there was no mention of it. Had I not seen the copy, I would not have known it existed in the house. I certainly had heard of the Bible and seen copies at church, but never read it nor owned my own copy. I remember that Dad's Bible was somewhat tattered, the pages had red edging, and it was a King James Version. After looking it over, I replaced it on the shelf and left the room. I never did ask Dad about it nor did I pick it up and read it for myself.

One incident that had a powerful impact on my life, and still does, took place one evening just after turning in for bed; my bedroom was just down the hall from Mom and Dad's room. While in my room, I realized I needed to get up for some reason—I think to use the bathroom. Stepping into the hallway, I glanced toward my parents' room and saw my Dad quietly kneeling, with his back to me and praying. I had never seen him do this before, so I just stood there and watched. A sense of reverence and awe came over me, and after a few moments, I headed to the washroom, not fully grasping what I had just witnessed. It was the first of many times I saw Dad on his knees at his bedside—I often wonder what he was praying about. There were also times after I found the Bible on Dad's nightstand, when I witnessed him laying in bed reading from this very book.

Dad was very quiet regarding what he believed about God and faith. I do not know if he had saving faith in Jesus Christ at the time. I do not ever remember him sharing the Gospel, sharing his faith, encouraging us to read the Bible, or reading the Bible or Bible stories to us, but his actions, including saying grace at the table every day before meals, planted seeds that began to set patterns in my life and would later take root. Through my observation of Dad, God began to make me aware of Himself, and I began, as a young person, kneeling beside my bed and praying to God. I remember very clearly my heartfelt prayer that I could be just like my Dad.

Mom, who had some connection with the church in the past (I am not sure which denomination), would come to church with us occasionally. From what I remember, Mom had mentioned that she had been hurt by something in the church sometime before, although I am not sure of the details. Despite that, Mom never spoke ill of the church or faith in general that I am aware of. Her support of Dad taking us to church, saying grace before meals, praying at his bedside, and reading from his Bible spoke volumes to me and reinforced the fact that there was something important about things of faith. Mom too was quiet about what her thoughts were about God; however, like Dad, through Mom, and her response to and support of Dad, God used them to make me aware of Himself.

One of the unique blessings we had as a family was the fact that we lived right beside my Mom's middle sister (my Aunt Janice) and her family. What made it special for me is that Aunt Janice had a son, my cousin, Peter—we were born two weeks apart. Though Peter was my cousin, I considered, and still do consider, him to be the brother I never

Spiritual Seeds (Part 1)

had. We spent much time together just hanging out, camping, going to the back woods, and spending time at Camp Samac (the local Boy Scout Camp) which had an Olympic-sized pool. I remember the numerous times we headed to the Camp when they (the Camp pool staff) organized midnight swims for the community. One memory, however, sticks out in my mind as to how God used Peter to plant a seed that God would use later in my life.

I remember being in the basement of his house as we were rummaging through some stuff, including magazines (*Sports Illustrated*) and comic books (Peter had a great collection of GI Joe comics). As I was leafing through one of the magazines, I noticed a picture of a teenager pressed against a tree encircled by other youth that looked around his age, one threatening with a shotgun. The picture was related to the title, *Left Behind,* which was later developed into a series of books written by Tim LaHaye (I had no idea who he was at the time) about a time called The Tribulation—an event that I was unfamiliar with. The picture created some uneasiness within me, but I do not remember saying anything about it. I switched to some other material and tried not to think about it, although that image would revisit my mind occasionally. That image embossed a major imprint in my mind that God used many years later to bring me to the point of calling out to Him to save me.

Having been raised in a home that identified with the Catholic Church, Mom and Dad registered us with the local Catholic Elementary School Board. Consequently, my elementary and junior high school days were spent within the Catholic system between two schools namely, St. Joseph School and Father Venini School (named after a priest who was martyred in Central America during the 1970s). During these years, knowledge of God, Jesus, and the true meaning of Christmas and Easter, was further reinforced through teachers, priests and nuns, school activities, assemblies, and Masses (which were held on a scheduled basis for the whole school to attend in the school gymnasium). I was, in a real sense, immersed in an educational environment that promoted Christian values, and that encouraged the living out of those values in everyday life through good works. My experiences in the school system at that time further taught me about the seriousness of church, respecting church leaders and workers (the Pope, priests, and nuns), reverence for things of God, conforming to the authority of the Church, and doing good works.

Despite the many positive influences being in the system had on me, which God used to make me more aware of Him, I do not recall during my eight years of being in that system ever being encouraged to read the Bible for myself or the importance of daily Bible reading. I do not remember my parents ever being encouraged by the school to read the Scriptures to me, nor was I ever taught the need for me to have a personal relationship with Jesus, and to welcome Him into my life to cleanse away my sin. I do remember that it was best to leave the teaching of what is in the Bible to the priest. Obedience to and reverence of the Pope seemed to be more important than obedience and reverence for Jesus Christ due, in part, I think, to the belief that the Pope was infallible (exempt from making an error) and what he said was to be listened and adhered to.

There was no teaching directing people to check the Bible for themselves to make sure that what they were

Spiritual Seeds (Part 1)

being taught was Biblical truth. Acts 17:11 speaks to the importance of fact-checking what a person is being taught. It states, *Now the Bereans were of more noble character than the Thessalonians, for they received the message with great eagerness and examined the Scriptures every day to see if what Paul said was true.* Church teaching and doctrine seemed to have had a more prominent place than what the Bible had to say. These things, along with my naiveté, I believe, helped contribute to me not understanding the Biblical teaching of what it meant to be saved and how one is to go about doing that. Although God did use my experiences during elementary and junior high school years, I still, at that point, did not truly understand what it meant, and what was involved in being a true follower of Jesus Christ. Head knowledge was not enough (as I found out years later) and I continued my way in spiritual blindness unaware of my state. But God was not done with me.

During the latter months of my grade eight year, my classroom teacher arranged a tour of the local high school (O'Neill Collegiate and Vocational Institute) to provide an introduction to high school life. I remember how excited, but nervous, I was. I felt it was a significant turning point in my schooling career. Elementary school now seemed childish—I was on my way to the big leagues of the education system! It turns out that this high school was the same one that my Mom attended during her high school years in the 1940s. In one sense, going to this school was in the family line even though my two older sisters attended the rival high school on the east side of the city—Eastdale Collegiate. I still remember the wild and emotional football games between these two schools.

I would have to say that I did generally enjoy my time at O'Neill. I would not say I was a Rhodes Scholar by any means. Academically, I slipped through by a thin thread in some subjects, particularly math, and had to go to summer school to upgrade my geography mark if I was to get credit for it toward graduation. Though I did struggle with some academic subjects, largely due to the fact I did not apply myself, I would say that my greatest enjoyment was physical education and playing team sports such as football. I also enjoyed the social aspect of school (though I was a quiet individual), spending time with friends, teammates, and learning how to navigate the few girlfriend relationships I had.

One interesting incident was when I met a guy at school whose name was Dave Williams. I was in a few classes with him. He was a confident and somewhat outgoing individual, but what made my meeting him interesting was when I learned that years before, unknown to me, his father and my father worked together at General Motors! I found out later, through Dad, that they worked together in the same office. He relayed the story that one day, Dave's dad came into his office complaining about chest pains and asked Dad if he would take him to the hospital. Dad did, and after being checked out by the doctor, he was given a clean bill of health. Sometime after returning to work, he collapsed. Dad sprang into action and administered Artificial Respiration (there was no such thing as CPR training at the time) to no avail, and Dave's dad passed away. That incident proved to be a natural connecting point for Dave and me and we became friends. I would never have known about how Dad tried to save Dave's dad's life, unless I had met Dave. Dad was never

Spiritual Seeds (Part 1)

one to draw attention to himself—it was an example of humility to me.

As a side note, Dad was also instrumental in saving a man from drowning by diving into a pool, bringing the man to the surface and to the pool deck, where he administered Artificial Respiration. He revived the man and he survived. My sister Janice told me of this incident many years later. Again, I would never have heard it from Dad. Another glimpse of the character of God, namely, humility.

Another incident at high school I remember took place one afternoon during lunch break. I headed down to the school cafeteria (something of the past) to have a bite to eat. The cafeteria was packed as usual with a noise level that would rival any hockey rink. One time a hamburger patty was launched through the air at someone seated at the other end of the room! I also remember the vending machines there. For the right amount of money you could enjoy pop, chips, or a yummy sticky bun. I never seemed to have enough change to access those goodies, so I had to settle for drooling at the thought of having one of them. The cafeteria was a great place to socialize and catch up with friends, and it was a good place to go to work on homework later in the afternoon after the lunch rush.

It was not only things like the flying hamburger patty that caught my attention, however. I remember one day during lunch break, sitting at my table with several people I knew, gazing around the room looking for other familiar faces. As I surveyed the room, I noticed a student sitting at another table surrounded by other students busily socializing with their friends. Whether he knew these other people I do not know, but despite the activity going on around him, he methodically laid his food out in front of him, bowed his head, and prayed. He did not appear rushed in doing so nor did he sneak a look around beforehand to see who might be watching him. He was very intentional and ended his prayer with a sign of the cross (something I was familiar with coming from a Catholic background). He seemed to show no concern about what other people might say to him or about him, about others noticing him, or the possibility of becoming the brunt of jokes and ridicule. He was one of the first people (in my age group) I witnessed living out their faith in public in the face of potential rejection from others. I can still picture that incident in my mind today. His action showed me that there was something real about faith; however, I soon went on with my usual day-to-day living without realizing that God was trying to get my attention.

At the end of grade eleven, I secured a job at Camp Samac Boy Scout Camp (for the second summer) on the maintenance crew, and was issued the coveted Camp Samac maintenance crew t-shirt. The Camp was located a short bike ride away from my house. It was a beautiful place to work and a great staff to work with and for. There were lots of trees, a lake, cabins, and beautiful trails. Our job responsibilities varied from garbage pick-up, landscaping, painting, shingling, outhouse cleaning (a gross job at times), and copious amounts of grass cutting.

One of my supervisors, the main boss, was named John Sealy. He was an older man, I think in his sixties, built like a bodybuilder. He had a rugged profile, had backbone, was a good leader, and had a gentle heart. One incident that sticks out in my mind was the time John and I were sitting in the old maintenance truck during a lull in work. I am not

Spiritual Seeds (Part 1)

sure how the subject came up, but John began to relay the story of how he became a Christian. He explained to me that he had a heart attack sometime before; consequently, he spent some recovery time in the hospital. While in his hospital bed, he was able to secure a copy of the Bible. I am not sure if someone brought it to him, or if it was a copy that was provided by the hospital at his request. Nevertheless, he had a copy in his hands. Compassionately and sincerely, John explained that while in his bed, he read from the Scriptures, through which he came to believe and place his faith in Jesus Christ. I just sat there and listened, politely nodding my head. I had heard of the term "Bible thumper" before, but it was always in a derogatory sense. Though I respected John, I may have thought he was one of "those." I don't remember saying much in response and continued in my delusion and hardness of heart; after all, I thought I was a Christian. I was a good person and tried to do good works and believed, because of that, I was good with God. Unbeknownst to me, God was slowly creating cracks in my hard-shelled, sin-veiled heart, working to remove the blinders from my eyes that were causing me not to see the truth. John was one of the first individuals I remember openly and unashamedly sharing his testimony with me, of how God changed his life through Christ. Sadly, a few years after John retired, I was told he died from a heart attack while shovelling his driveway.

In June 1977, I walked the school stage to receive my grade twelve diploma. It was a great feeling to have that sense of achievement and freedom from four years of academic responsibilities, and with that, the excitement of a new chapter in my life. I was now free to pursue my dreams, of which I had no idea what direction to go given the variety of interests I had. My head was certainly full of dreams, things that were exciting possibilities, some which were not realistic, but it was still fun to dream. I wanted to be a bush pilot, a soldier, a police officer, an electrician, a mechanic, a pipefitter, and a doctor. The possibilities seemed endless. You name it, and I likely wanted to consider being it.

After graduation, the work search began in earnest. I applied to a variety of places, one of which was a place called Cadburys, a chocolate bar factory in Whitby, Ontario. I remember the interview quite well. After being asked several standard interview questions, to which I responded as well as I could, the interviewer asked me if I had any questions I would like to ask him. I remember saying, "Whether I get the job or not, how do you get the caramel in the caramilk?" He and I started to chuckle, and he proceeded to explain the top-secret, highly sensitive procedure. After the interview, I left and went home, setting my sights on other possibilities thinking that the interview was a colossal fail. Within a few hours, the gentleman called and offered me the job!

I officially began work as a Cadbury's employee in September of 1977, and was there until the beginning of October the same year—about one month in all. During one shift, I was put in charge of washing out the bins they used to put chocolate bar wafers in. The process involved going outside the building to access a water hose that was hooked up to hot water—very hot water! As I turned the tap on, the pressure of the water swung the hose around and I was hit square in the chest with a blast. I ended up in the first-aid station with first degree burns. Fortunately, they did not blister, and it did not take long before I healed up.

Spiritual Seeds (Part 1)

I met some nice people while at the factory and got a bit of a taste of what it was like to work full-time as a non-student. Though I did generally enjoy my time there, and the pay was reasonable—actually more than what I had been paid in previous summer jobs, I felt restless and did not embrace the idea of doing this kind of work for a living. I was looking for something else, but I did not exactly know what that was. Consequently, I quit my job and enrolled in night school at the local college, Durham College, to pursue academic upgrading in biology and chemistry with no idea where that would take me. I just needed something to occupy my time and give me a sense of purpose and direction; I was still living at home at the time.

Searching for a job was still a priority. During this time, I was made aware of an opportunity with the Hudson's Bay Company which was in the process of opening a new department store in the local Oshawa Shopping Centre (a place where my cousin Peter and I spent many hours hanging out during our teenage years). It was worth a try so I applied, not knowing whether my chances would be very good; however, I was called for an interview. As a result, I was hired part-time and began work as a salesman in the sporting goods department in about October of the same year I left Cadburys.

Sales was never really my forte. I remember a few years before working at Hudson's Bay, my Mom and Dad knew some people who were involved with Amway (a door-to-door sales company). One time, when our family was visiting them, I got the sales pitch and was lured into buying my starter kit of goodies to sell. One of our neighbours, who lived behind us, seemed like a good place to start, so I hesitantly headed over to their place hoping to make my very first sale. As I reached their back door, I recall thinking to myself, "What am I doing?" I was nervous and a little doubtful that this was the gold mine I was hoping to strike. I knocked on the door, I am not sure how loud, and waited briefly to see if someone would come. I waited for about two minutes. To my relief, no one came, so I quickly backed down the stairs, headed for home, and permanently retired as an Amway salesman. As for the starter kit—I used up the product on myself. So much for door-to-door sales!

Working in the sporting goods department at the Bay did have some perks, however. One of them was that we were able to get firsthand viewing of new products that were coming on the market and, if interested, could get first shot at buying them with a staff discount. It was also a time, though not a perk, to observe people's interactions with others, some which were commendable, and some that were very inconsiderate and rude. It was a lesson in how some people had no regard for how their actions and words negatively impacted those who were on the receiving end. They were more concerned with getting what they wanted, even if it meant stomping on other people. It was something I was not used to and was definitely not something I saw in my parents, siblings, or John Sealy. There was a difference in them.

In the summer of 1978, while I was still in the employ of Hudson's Bay Company, I applied for acceptance, for the coming fall, into the Sports Administration program at Durham College. I was accepted! It was exciting to have the opportunity to go on to post-secondary schooling in a subject area that perked my interest, but in reality, deep down, I was wandering and was not sure what I really

Spiritual Seeds (Part 1)

wanted to pursue. This seemed like a good start, however. The program itself was two years in length and was not work-intensive. It was not long into the program that I realized I did not have a very good sense of where this area of study would lead. I did, however, enjoy meeting the people I did and those I studied with. One student in our program, by the name of Tom McCarthy, played for the Oshawa Generals (the local Jr. 'A' hockey club) at the time, and was later drafted by the Minnesota North Stars of the NHL.

College was a place to study but also a place to socialize and party, which I did occasionally take part in, but in all of that, I still had a sense of emptiness and lack of clear direction. I came to the decision, near the end of my first year, that I would quit the program. I did so, completing my first year, and turned to focus on my part-time job at the Bay.

After some time on the floor, working part-time in sales, the opportunity came up to transfer to the shipping and receiving department for a full-time position, so I submitted my name for transfer and my transfer was approved! Off I went skipping to the loading docks and I loved it! I enjoyed my fellow dock-hands and interacting with the truck drivers. The job was physical in nature, which I loved, and allowed me to get to know other employees that worked in the various departments around the store. I remember one time when we received a shipment that included some sporting goods. In the shipping container were brand new hockey sticks. Gary, my boss, and I proceeded to release a couple of them from the bondage of the container and broke out into a rowdy game of hockey on the loading dock. While running around, body-checking each other into boxes, cheering, and blasting shots at one another, the top dog of the Hudson's Bay Company, from Toronto I believe, walked through the loading dock doors with our store manager who was giving him a store tour! Gary and I froze. Dumbfounded we just stared at the two of them anticipating, in our minds, that we would be issued our pink slips on the spot. To our amazement the top dog asked, "Who's winning boys?" We responded with a nervous chuckle and they left. We never heard anything more about it, not even from our store manager! But we never did that again! In hindsight, the top dog's, and our manager's, response to our activities was a demonstration of what grace looks like. Though they could have, they did not give us what we deserved and let us off the hook. A lesson I would learn later in life regarding God and His gracious mercy which He was offering to me.

During that winter, Gary and I came up with a money-making scheme that, in our minds, would provide us with some extra cash to add to our present wages. As a result, we came up with a snow removal business plan. We figured we would provide snow removal from people's driveways for a seasonal cost—I think we charged about fifteen dollars for a half-season and thirty for the whole season (our lack of business sense began to shine through!). We were not businessmen! We spent more money getting to people's houses than what we brought in through customers. My Dad, in his genuine willingness to help, even printed up, at work, promotional posters for our business with a logo picturing someone cleaning a driveway with a snow blower. Because we did not have the money to buy a snowblower, all our snow removal

Spiritual Seeds (Part 1)

was done by shovel! I would say the poster was innocently misleading, but the picture was cool.

I remember getting an early morning phone call at home, one that interrupted my anticipated sleep-in, from a customer complaining that we had not been over to their place to clear their driveway. I responded by saying, "It isn't my fault it snowed!" Dad just shook his head as he listened from the kitchen. I would say my PR skills were still in the development stage; fortunately, it did not snow much that season! We did go over and clear their driveway, but shortly after that our hair-brained business scheme fell by the wayside and we thought it better to focus on making money via our jobs at the Bay.

The job at the Bay ticked on and around the spring of that year (1980), my parents mentioned that I should contact my cousins, who had moved to Fort McMurray (Fort Mac), Alberta, about the possibility of work out there. Through my parents, I found out that my cousins, Brian and Mary Dobbs, worked for a big oil company called Syncrude, which had an operation going north of Fort Mac. I took my parent's advice and called them from work. Through my conversations with them, it was arranged that I would head west that summer, in line with the adage, "Go west young man," and take up residence with my cousins. In June, I resigned from the Bay and boarded a flight, the first time I had ever set foot on a passenger jet—an Air Canada 737 to be exact—and headed to Edmonton International Airport. This was a new step in my life in that I was now beginning to strike out on my own—in a sense moving out from the familiar, often taken for granted benefits and security of home, at age nineteen, to carve a path in the world for myself.

I was a bit nervous embarking on this new adventure, having rarely spent time with my cousins when they lived in the Toronto area, but looked forward to finally seeing what it was like out West and getting to know them better. I remember the plane banking around to line up for the runway in Edmonton and the sound of the wheels as they touched down, my anticipation building as to what I might see when I made it to my destination. After deplaning, I headed for the luggage pick-up area and then bought a bus ticket for the four-hour trip to Fort McMurray on the Red Arrow Express—a bus decked out with a fridge at the back, which passengers could access for water, etc. and a washroom to boot. It was pretty luxurious compared to the public transportation I was used to riding on back home in Ontario.

The bus left the Edmonton terminal in the evening and arrived in Fort McMurray in the wee hours of the morning. My cousins arrived to pick me up, after I called to let them know I had arrived, and whisked me off to their home—112 Marten Place—located on a hill area just after the bridge spanning the Athabasca River. Upon arrival at their home, I remember my cousins, Brian and Mary's kids (Carl, Jeff, Stacey, and Kim), sitting on the living room couch waiting to meet and greet me. It was almost like coming home in the way they warmly accepted me into their home and family. After visiting for a while, it was off to bed with thoughts of a job search the next day.

Brian and Mary were very helpful in guiding me as to where I could look for job postings in the area, and encouraged me to contact the local employment office. I did so, and they gave me a ride down to their office, where I took

Spiritual Seeds (Part 1)

a seat with many other job seekers. Before long, one of the employees approached me and said that a person who had been hired for the summer at Syncrude, had backed out and would I like the job! That was a no-brainer! I began my employment in the Material Services Department at the Syncrude Refinery, north of Fort McMurray. I am sure my feet did not hit the ground walking out of that office! It was an exciting relief that I got a job—and quickly at that. "Was this just coincidence, being at the right place at the right time, or did Brian and Mary put a good word in for me? Or, was there a bigger hand behind it all?" I casually wondered.

Syncrude was HUGE! And I was somewhat overwhelmed with the size of the place. I remember standing beside one of the big dump truck's (a Euclid) tires. My shoulder was even with the middle of the tire and each tire had its own separate transmission! My job assignment was to evaluate and assess heavy equipment implements to see whether or not they were serviceable and able to be put back into active service. It was an interesting job, a little monotonous at times, but it paid well, and I met some great people, both students and full-time career employees.

One of the perks of my position was that I was temporarily assigned my own pick-up truck to use. One time, during a lull, I decided to drive out to the dump just outside of the refinery site to watch the grizzly bears. When I arrived at the site, I noticed two of them playfully batting each other around just behind a mound of dirt at the rim of the dump pit. In my curious naiveté, I jumped out of my truck and climbed the ridge to get a closer look. As I was climbing, another fellow called out to me and said, "Who is your next of kin, because those bears are waiting for you on the other side of that mound!" Needleless to say, no further warnings were needed, as I hustled down back into my truck, leaving the pit feeling quite foolish. It was, and could have been a tragic, lesson in thinking before acting.

I remember one time, while on shift, needing to go to one of the Syncrude departments to see about borrowing a forklift. I came across some rather crusty individuals, but there was one that stuck out in my mind in particular. He was probably, by my estimation, in his early thirties and blended in, in terms of his persona. In other words, he appeared to be cut from the same cloth as those who were free with their colourful language, gruffness, and seeming desire to display a macho (over-testosteroned) exterior. What stuck out in my mind, was that I came across this same individual, who lived in the same neighbourhood as Brian and Mary, as he was walking with his family. He did not acknowledge me, even though he recognized me from Syncrude. He seemed to want to avoid me and appeared quite different, at least on the outside, from the way he presented himself at work. He did not emulate any appearance of a rough character in any way, at least from outside appearances. This created a paradox for me. I began to ask myself, "Is this the same person I saw at work? Who is this person when no one is looking? Is he one kind of person at work and another at home? Should not who we truly are be evident in all settings including home and work? Who is the real person?" I later asked these same questions about those who claimed to be religious or claimed some form of faith.

As the summer was drawing closer to an end, and though there was the opportunity to travel to Finland or

Spiritual Seeds (Part 1)

Saudi Arabia to work in the oil fields there, I felt the desire to go back to school. Consequently, I applied to the University of Alberta hoping to gain acceptance into their Physical Education program. After several calls to the admissions office, things did not look very promising, so I contacted the admissions office at the University of Western Ontario (UWO), in London, Ontario, to reactivate my application which I had submitted sometime before heading out west. In a short time, UWO accepted my application into the Physical Education program. No sooner had they done so, then I received a call from U of A that they also had accepted me, but my decision was made and I headed back east to begin my first semester of studies. My post-secondary education journey away from home had begun.

Spiritual Seeds (Part 2)

The reactivation of my application to UWO came in a timely fashion in that it provided me a much-needed window to get student loans in place and arrange for a place to stay. Fortunately, my eldest sister Kara, her husband Jim, and their two kids—Aaron and Sarah—lived just outside of London, Ontario, about a half-hour drive to the University campus. They offered their place very willingly and were quite happy with me moving in with them while I attended school. This also meant that my living expenses would be much less than what they would have been had I stayed in residence on campus. It also lent itself to a more conducive setting to apply myself to school studies rather than getting wrapped up in the party scene. I had a lot of fun living at their place. We had lots of laughs and good discussions around the table—time that I will always cherish with my oldest sister and her family.

In my circle of religious influence at that time, I came away with the sense that the true church was the Catholic Church and that those who called themselves "Evangelical" were people who were uninformed and to be avoided. I also recall, through discussion and observation, there seemed to be an emphasis on good works to find favour with God, and a reliance on the Pope (as the authority in spiritual matters). Through him, priests and the Church were designated as the authoritative interpreters of Scripture. There was no encouragement, nor teaching of the need for people to read and study the Scriptures for themselves, to see whether or not what they were being taught was backed up by the Word of God—the same views, attitudes, and practices originally observed as I grew up while attending church as a younger person. As a result, I accepted these practices and attitudes (particularly concerning "Evangelicals") as truth. It seemed that this was the way life worked regarding faith, religion, and spiritual matters.

Not long into my first year, I found myself sitting outside the gymnasium, in one of the university buildings, feeling somewhat lonely having not met many people at that point. As I sat there watching the crowd pass by, my eye caught a familiar face working her way through the crowd. I recognized this girl from the High School I attended but did not know her name. Out of character, I stepped in front of her and said, "I know you! You went to O'Neill Collegiate." She responded with "Yes" followed by conversation during which I found out her name—Debbie Austin. I do not remember what was said, or for how long we spoke, but by the end of our conversation it was arranged that we would get together for a game of

Spiritual Seeds (Part 2)

squash later that week. It was not long after our first squash game that our seeing each other became more serious, so much so that it led to our marriage engagement in December that year (about four months after we met!).

Debbie was also from Oshawa, Ontario, and her relatives, who mostly lived in St. Catherines, Ontario, came from a Salvation Army church background. Debbie's immediate family, her Mom, Dad, and three siblings, to my knowledge, were not connected with a church home. Because I came from a Catholic background, we planned to be married in the Catholic Church I attended while growing up. Consequently, it was required by the Catholic Church that Debbie convert to Catholicism. At the time, I did not understand nor question the reason for this and just accepted that it needed to be done. Debbie willingly agreed and we began that process while both of us were still attending school. The catechism classes we sat in seemed to focus mostly on church doctrine (e.g., the Virgin Mary, the rosary, the seven sacraments that lead to salvation, etc.), and what we were taught we just accepted as being true. As I look back, I am not surprised that I would accept what I heard through church authority (the priests) as truth, because I was never taught the importance of looking into the Scriptures myself to see if what I was being taught was actually what God said—an unfortunate position many people find themselves in today.

I remember that, through the Catholic student office on campus, a retreat called Antioch II had been arranged to which we were invited. It was to be held at a retreat centre out in the countryside beyond city limits. I had never attended nor experienced anything like this before, so it was foreign to me and made me a little nervous. I do not recall all of the things we did or what was taught, but I do remember, as part of the retreat closing activities, we had a chapel where we had a speaker and some singing. At the end of the chapel, we were all given wooden cross necklaces to wear and have as a keepsake. Everyone was hugging each other, and were laughing, and smiling—it was a very warm atmosphere and we left feeling rather at peace. On the way back to campus to drop Debbie off at her residence, I stopped off at a bank close to the university. After doing what I needed to do, I returned to the vehicle. As I backed out, I recognized a guy in another vehicle who I had just previously seen at the retreat. All I remember is that, for whatever reason, he gave me a look like he would bite my head off if he had the opportunity. The interesting thing was this was the same guy, who maybe an hour or so ago, was part of everyone hugging and wishing each other well at the retreat. Again, the paradox presented itself to me; there seemed to be a superficiality to all of this. In my thought processes at the time, I asked, "What impact had been made on this guy's life after attending the retreat? Should not his response have been more gracious whether or not he was having a bad day? Did what happened at the retreat have any impact outside of the retreat centre? Was his religious experience only reserved for certain locations and times? Did all that catechism and teaching have any importance on the way a person carried themselves in public and private life?" These questions continued to be unanswered.

I remember going to visit Debbie at her residence located off-campus at Huron College, which was affiliated with the University and the Anglican Church. As I walked the halls by myself, I noticed an office door slightly ajar

Spiritual Seeds (Part 2)

enough that, as I approached, I could get a glimpse inside. As I glanced, my eye immediately caught the sight of a minister with head bowed at his desk, praying. There was something genuine and real about it, not fake or superficial—and I wanted a piece of that! That image ingrained itself in my mind, and even at that point in my life, I told Debbie that I was wondering about entering the ministry! That idea, however, fizzled out after a short time.

Debbie and I were married in August of 1981 and moved into our first apartment on campus. While at the apartment, we opened our extra bedroom to a fellow student by the name of Glen Sweazy, to help with rent. We found out he participated in the 1976 Olympics as a race walker. He stayed with us for a short time and then moved out to his own place. He was an interesting individual, but we did not have many opportunities to really get to know one another due to our busy school schedules.

One of the wedding gifts we were given, was a Catholic Bible. That Bible was neatly placed on a table for display in the living room, rarely opened, read, or studied—it was primarily on display. I do not recall any time that Debbie and I purposefully studied (though we may have read it time to time) or talked about the Bible together in those early married years. Neither one of us seemed to see the importance of searching the Scriptures for ourselves. Checking off going to church, being a good person, relying on the pastor or priest's sermon, and doing good works seemed to be all that was needed.

An opportunity presented itself to move from our apartment into a townhouse across the parking lot, which would provide us with more living space. We applied, and our application was accepted, so we moved into our new abode toward the end of our first year of university. To help with rent, since our first experience with Glen Sweazy was a positive one, we inquired about fellow students who were looking for a place to stay. A fellow by the name of Rob Aquilina expressed interest. He seemed like a good candidate, so we invited him to come and stay with us. As we got to know Rob, I learned that he was quite involved with North Park Chapel, a Protestant church located within the city. He played on their ball team and wanted to be involved as a Sunday school teacher.

I remember one evening when Rob invited a fellow by the name of Bruce (I forget his last name), an older student (in his thirties), over to our place so they could have a chat. Bruce seemed to be involved in recruiting Sunday school teachers for the church. I remember watching and listening, from a distance, to their conversation and the questions Bruce was asking him about his faith. This was unusual to me as I had never witnessed this before. I never said anything, but just observed, listened to Rob's responses, and then watched Rob as he carried out everyday life while living with us. He was genuine and real about his faith. He was not pushy about it and was not hiding it, nor afraid that others knew about it. He shared with me that one time, while at home, his father responded to his faith in a negative way, but that did not shake his convictions.

Rob invited us to his church, which we attended a couple of times. The teaching was somewhat different from what I was used to, and people brought their own Bibles! This was indeed different! We also were invited for lunch by Rob's friend's family, where I got a taste of what church fellowship was like. People did not just leave the

Spiritual Seeds (Part 2)

service and get on with their own thing; they actually took time to visit and spend time together—not in a hurry to get away from each other! They seemed genuinely interested in and caring for one another.

One day, when I was home alone, two young men showed up at our door. They were neatly dressed, each with a white shirt and dress pants. I do not remember the initial words spoken, but I ended up inviting them in to hear what they had to say. I do not recall them speaking much about what the Bible said. They seemed to be more focused on getting a copy of the particular book they had brought into my hands. They mostly spoke while I politely listened, at the end of which they presented me with their book. The book was about a man by the name of Joseph Smith, who seemed to be an important character in their belief system. I accepted, mostly because I had listened enough, and then bid them farewell as they went on their way. I placed the book on the upper shelf of one of the closets thinking I might look at it later. What struck me was that this book seemed to be more important to them than the Bible (in stark contrast to what I had observed with Rob, our roommate); consequently, I never did read the book and eventually threw it out. I learned later that these gentlemen were associated with the Mormons.

On October 12, 1982, our first daughter, Julianna, was born. I remember being in the delivery room helping Debbie with her breathing and coaching her through the process, all the while with doctors, nurses, and medical interns milling around—it was a teaching hospital. Debbie's mother had driven down from Oshawa to help with things at our home and was at the hospital in the waiting room. As Julianna broke through into this world I was overwhelmed with emotion. After I welcomed and beheld our first child, and checking to make sure Deb was fine, I went to the waiting room to announce Julianna's birth. Before I could get the words out, I began to weep uncontrollably, having just witnessed the incredible miracle of life. This was indeed a miracle I beheld, and I was overwhelmed and in awe. Three more times, after having moved from London, Ontario, I had that blessing and privilege to see our children being given the breath of life and entering this world. I had an extra big smile when we were blessed with our son, Patrick, two years later. I wonder how my Dad felt inside when he realized a son had been born to him as well back in 1959. Caitlin and Emilie (my little grasshopper), two of our other bundles of joy, were born in 1987 and 1989 respectfully.

Not long after Julianna was born, I noticed a hernia had developed on the opposite side of my groin area. I had had a previous hernia repaired when I was eighteen and it looked like I was headed back to the body shop for another repair job. I arranged an appointment at Shouldice Hospital, located in Thornhill, Ontario, for a consultation, after which I hoped to get scheduled for surgery. Shouldice, I found out the first time I was there, was world-renowned for their expertise in hernia repair. I had heard of this place through a friend of my Dad, Nelson Brown, who himself had been a patient there. I remember him saying that they served breaded hernias to the patients for breakfast—he was quite the comic! After my consultation, the surgery date was set, and I made preparations for the big day.

Shouldice looked more like a hotel than a hospital, was very welcoming, and calming to anyone hesitant or ner-

Spiritual Seeds (Part 2)

vous about having surgery. I remember arriving the day before my surgery to check in and get settled into my room, which I shared with another individual. My roommate was a bit older than me and shared with me that he was getting married soon. He talked about making a prenuptial agreement (something I had never heard of before) with his fiancé which was designed to lay out ahead of time, in the event of a divorce, how things would be split up between them. I thought this quite odd as it seemed like they were already setting themselves up to believe that divorce was inevitable, but I did not feel it was my place to say anything at that point.

Around the same time, another individual wandered in, a fellow about the same age as my roommate. He shared his story of how he had left his wife, seeking after other things and women. His wife told him that whether or not he returned, though she desired that he would, she would continue to pray for him, that she loved him, and encouraged him not to turn his back on God. He said, in a very sincere and heartfelt manner, that he was so moved by his wife's response that he returned to his wife, and they were now living happily together again. He explained how God had impacted his life. My roommate was stunned; I sat there listening and digesting what was said—still believing that I was already in God's good books. By the end of the conversation, my roommate was debating whether a prenuptial agreement was even necessary. I wonder what direction that man's life took after leaving Shouldice Hospital that week?

Well, the time came for the duty nurse to do her rounds and administer sleeping pills to the ones having surgery the next morning of which I was one. It was not long before I was fast asleep. No sooner, it seemed, had I gulped down the pill, the orderlies were wheeling me down the hall to the elevator, and then the operating room. Still quite groggy, I remember the surgeons talking real estate and other stuff as they worked on me; I was only given a local anesthetic. It was another day at the office for those guys! Before I knew it, all stapled-up and ready to go, I was on the way back to my room for recovery.

After some time sleeping off the effects of the sleeping pill, as well as the surgery, the nurses came around encouraging me, I should say that lightly, to get up and start walking around. It was slow at first, but after a day or two, things began to loosen up a bit. Not far from my room was a lounge with a pool table and a comfortable sitting area furnished with couches and chairs. It was here that I had the opportunity to meet some of the other patients that were housed on my floor. You could clearly tell we were all hernia patients by our distinctive walk. It was a no-no to laugh unless you wanted some discomfort; consequently, the challenge was on to try to make each other laugh. Several times I had to support my incision area as I succumbed to the plethora of jokes circulating around.

One of the patients I met was a man by the name of Royce Owens, a Vietnam War veteran who served in the United States Navy. He was from South Carolina and it was not long before I saw that he was a man of faith (in word and action). He was not pushy, but sincere and genuine, and unashamed in his sharing of what God had done in his life. He was a gentleman and very easy to converse with. We, as a group, so much appreciated him that we

Spiritual Seeds (Part 2)

encouraged him to lead a church service for us. He appeared a little uncomfortable with that, so it did not come to fruition. By the time it came for us to pack up to go, a group of us, including Royce, had developed a close bond and it was difficult to say goodbye. Goodbye it was, however, as we said farewell to each other and the staff of the Hernia Hotel and headed our separate ways.

Back on campus in London, Ontario, Debbie and I, because we were in our final year of studies, began looking into applying to several different teacher's colleges for the coming fall. In the process of our search, we applied to several colleges in the province, but the response was either "No" or only one of us was granted acceptance. It was not until we applied to Brock University, located on the Niagara Escarpment in the St. Catherines' area, that we both were granted entrance into their teacher training program. I remember that, at the time we were looking for teacher's colleges to attend, I had secured a summer job with McCormick's which was a cookie and ice cream cone factory. It was a cool job and had its perks, such as access to those delicious sugar cones whenever the hunger pangs struck.

Through working at McCormick's, one of my coworkers offered to help us move to St. Catherines at the end of the summer. When the time came, he backed out at the last minute and left us in an awkward situation. In response, my Dad, with no hesitation, drove from Oshawa to London, a two-and-a-half hour drive, to step in and help us move; my brother-in-law Jim also offered his time. Dad drove a small van and soon realized the move was going to take longer than expected; consequently, and without hesitation, Dad called in to work and said he would not be in.

Jim also gave of his time late into the evening, knowing he had to work the next day. We moved our belongings through the night, and in the wee hours of the morning of the next day, we completed transporting our worldly belongings into our apartment in St. Catherines, not many days before we were to begin classes.

Dad's and Jim's willingness to help despite their own responsibilities, which placed them in a rather inconvenient situation, spoke volumes. Helping us was a cost to them and they willingly paid that cost in time, loss of sleep, and muscle power. It was a lesson in selflessness, putting others' needs ahead of one's own, and a willingness to pay the cost and price for our benefit—a lesson in self-sacrifice I would later fully understand concerning the price Jesus Christ paid for you and me when He went to the cross at Calvary.

St. Catherines was a city with a small-town feel. The people were friendly, and we had access to all the amenities we needed. The university itself was in a beautiful area on the outer rim of the city, and the teacher's college had a student enrollment small enough that meaningful connections could be made. One of the benefits of being in St. Catherines was the nearness of Deb's relatives. They also lived in the city and were always willing to help look after Julianna when Debbie and I had to attend classes. Most of her relatives were regular Salvation Army Church attendees, either involved in teaching Sunday school and/or attending services.

I remember one time when Deb's aunt and uncle took us to their church for a quick tour. After meeting the minister, I wandered into the sanctuary where they held services. Out of curiosity, I went up on the platform to look at

Spiritual Seeds (Part 2)

what material was on the pulpit to see what the minister was preaching about—the only thing there was a Bible. In hindsight, my motive for doing this was rather arrogant. I did this to compare what they were teaching from to see whether it measured up to what I was familiar with in the Catholic Church.

Deb's grandparents, on both sides, were very godly people and had us over to their places for meals and visits. I remember many times sitting in the TV room with Deb's grandfather, watching TV and having discussions about what life was like for him growing up. Their Bible was always on the table beside the couch—and it was not there just for display. Though I may not have realized it at the time, God used their testimony of faith, as well as other relatives, to gently remind me that He was there. But at that point, I still saw myself as one of them—a Christian.

On several occasions, we attended church at the Salvation Army with Deb's family. I really enjoyed these services and noticed that they too were teaching directly from the Bible (like at North Park Chapel); the pastor-led prayers were also from the heart and not from a prescribed book of prayer. It seemed like the person praying knew Jesus personally, like He was their friend. Their prayers were not robotic, and they were genuine in opening up with their fears and requests to God. "Was it possible to know God like that?" I asked myself, "or was He a God who was far removed from people—a Person people just hoped would answer their prayers and look after them?" These were the same kind of questions I began to entertain while attending Rob Aquilina's church back in London, Ontario.

Another thing foreign to me was the *mercy seat* at the front of the sanctuary, which I found out later was designated for people who wanted to come forward to accept Christ as their Saviour, or if they had a burden they wanted to bring forward for people to pray for. I wondered, "What is this all about and why did it seem that this was so new to me?"

One day, Debbie and I decided to head down to the local mall and do some browsing and shopping. While there, we noticed several booths set up offering a variety of goods and services. One was occupied by a person who called themselves a psychic. Deb was intrigued and decided to go and have a chat with her. Afterward, Deb shared with me the things that the psychic said (I do not remember all the details), though what was said caused me to sense something was wrong with the whole thing. Somewhere along the line, I was made aware of the fact that Satan (the devil) can use tactics such as presenting lies mixed in with truth so that the lie will be believed as truth (John 8:44). I am not sure where I learned this. It could have been through previous discussions with Deb's relatives, while attending church, or in something I may have read; nonetheless, I believe God used that incident to reinforce the reality of the devil and spiritual warfare.

Our apartment was small but sufficient for our family; the building itself was quite large. On the upper floor lived a couple around our age, with their young one, who we met shortly after moving into our apartment. Their names were Colin and Theresa. Colin and Theresa were wonderful people and there was an immediate connection, once we had established that we all had familiarity with the Catholic Church.

Theresa was a person of conviction and backbone; Colin was the same, though in a quiet way. They too had

Spiritual Seeds (Part 2)

a Catholic Bible set on their coffee table, but there was something different. Though they affiliated themselves with being Catholic, their Bible was not just a display item. They took the initiative and read and studied the Bible for themselves! Though they respected and were not derogatory toward Church authority, they did not blindly accept what the priest said, nor did they consider the Pope as the ultimate authority on spiritual matters. They also did not consider the adherence to ritual as a way of sanctification (holiness) and finding favour with God—they knew and looked to Jesus and His Word as the ultimate authority. Their views (looking to the Bible and Jesus Christ as the final authority) were like those I had met who attended the Salvation Army church and North Park Chapel! "How could this be?" I thought. Although I was challenged by this, I still felt that I was somehow right with God. It was interesting to me that these people, including Deb's relatives, did not fit the profile or assumptions of those who would call them "Evangelicals," or "Bible Thumpers." These people displayed a genuine faith in Christ and what He had to say in the Bible, and were not ashamed to be identified as His followers. They found their identity in Christ, not in a denomination.

    One day, I was heading out from the apartment to do an errand in town. As I usually did, I hopped on the elevator for the ride down to the bottom floor and then went off to my vehicle. This time, however, when I boarded the elevator, I was surprised to see two other individuals inside (a young woman and man)—I had the elevator to myself most times. No sooner did the elevator door close, the young man turned to me and politely asked, "Do you know Jesus?" Immediately I went on guard and felt a little bit of defensiveness rise within me. I responded by saying, "I am a Christian," but inside I was asking myself, "Why is this guy asking me this? Of course, I am a Christian! I read the Bible (occasionally), go to church, and try to live a respectful life I thought!" I was hedging on the side of being somewhat insulted by the whole thing! The interesting thing was, I never answered the question he asked me. He did not ask me what church I went to or if I attended church. He did not ask me what my opinion was regarding some issue. No, he simply asked me, "Do you know Jesus?" Not, did I know *about* Jesus, but did I *know* Jesus? He was really asking me if I had a personal relationship with Jesus and I did not answer him by my reply. He must have sensed my defensiveness, so he did not press me further.

I thought my answer was sufficient, but I couldn't answer his question for two reasons. The first was that, in hindsight, I would consider myself at that time as a religious moralist. In other words, I was religious in that I knew about God and Jesus, read the Bible, prayed, went to church, and was familiar with Christian lingo. I was a moralist in that I tried to do good works, be kind to people, and strive to live a clean life. Secondly, I was blinded by my self-righteousness and, because of that, did not see the need for me to seek Jesus the way these people did. I felt I was already in the good books with God because of my religious moralism. I did not answer his question. Instead, I just said I was a Christian.

Another incident occurred later that week, not long after the meeting on the elevator. One evening, I was sitting in the living room of our apartment when there was a knock at the door; I got up and answered. There, standing

Spiritual Seeds (Part 2)

in front of me, was a young girl about ten years old, with an expression on her face that indicated she wanted to ask me something. She proceeded to ask me if I would be interested in reading a booklet she had outstretched in her little hand, called the *Watchtower*. As she was talking, I glanced down the hall to see a man leaning against the wall as if to stay out of sight. This seemed odd, and I sensed a little anger welling up in me. I politely declined the little girl's offer, glancing back at the man (who had obviously sent the girl to our door), giving him an unappreciative glance, and closed the door. I detected something was wrong with this picture. I felt as though I was being manipulated, that the girl was being used as a form of bait for me to take the publication. I was not impressed. "Why did the man not come to the door with the little girl rather than trying to stay out of my view?" It seemed so dishonest and manipulative. Upon later investigation, I realized they were associated with Jehovah's Witness. The question came to mind: "If this was a legitimate thing, why did they feel they had to go about presenting themselves the way they did and take a cloak and dagger approach?" I became very wary, guarded, and cautious after that.

It appeared to me, upon later reflection, that every time I was presented with an opportunity to hear teaching from the Bible, encouragement to read and study the Bible, and hear the witness of genuine believers, there came along people or material to entice me with a different gospel—one contradictory to the Bible; in some cases Truth mixed with error. It was reminiscent of what Jesus taught through the parable of the sower in Matthew 13, specifically, where He says, *When anyone hears the message about the kingdom and does not understand it, the evil one [Satan] comes and snatches away what was sown in his heart* (Matthew 13:19). In hindsight, I believe that had happened to me; there was indeed a real battle going on between Truth and falsehood and Satan did not want me to come to know the Truth.

After the required one year of study at Brock's Teacher's College, the day of graduation, in the spring of 1984, finally came. We were officially declared teachers, to be set loose on the youth of Ontario and become members of the Ontario Teacher's Federation. With hopeful anticipation, we prepared to move back to our birth city of Oshawa to seek employment with the local school board there.

Spiritual Seeds (Part 3)

Moving, for me, usually brought a sense of excitement and anticipation, and our move from St. Catherines back to Oshawa was no different. We carefully packed all our meager possessions, but had one item that needed to be attended to before we could hand in our apartment key. We owned a waterbed which was very comfortable to sleep on, especially in the winter, as it contained heated water, but there was a problem. How do we empty a waterbed when we lived on the fourth floor? The mattress was too heavy to drag to the tub and it was too cumbersome to drain by hose from the bedroom to the bathroom—what were we to do? "Ah hah," I thought! "I will attach the hose to the bed mattress, which was just a big water bladder, feed it out of our bedroom window, and try to avoid the windows of the apartments below us!" And so, I did. I fed the hose out the window, until it had stretched out its length, and then let loose the water valve.

Fortunately, everything held. I do not know if I really thought through what other people might think or say, let alone whether people would even notice a twenty-five foot hose hanging out of the fourth-story window about twenty feet from the ground. There is no question it did not go unnoticed, but no one said anything. After the deed was done, we packed up the bed, and Deb (who was well into her second pregnancy), Julianna, and I, including the cat we originally snuck into our apartment in a gym bag, set sail for Oshawa.

It was exciting to be heading back to familiar territory and dreaming about the potential of securing our first teaching jobs. We, of course, did not have a place to live right away and in light of that, my Mom and Dad offered their place to lay our heads until we were able to get our feet on the ground and find our own abode. Neither one of us had work lined up at the time. Consequently, Dad knew a guy who operated a courier business (Elite Courier) who required another driver. I applied and got the job. It was great! I was now able to generate some income, pay bills, and buy things that we needed. Although most of my deliveries were within the Oshawa area, I remember doing one trip to downtown Toronto. While driving on Highway 401, which is an experience in itself, the master brake cylinder on the delivery van began to fail, which made braking a bit of a challenge to say the least. To come to a stop, I had to pump that brake pedal like I was working the pump handle on a sink, but it worked. I did so all the way back to Oshawa after completing my delivery. That was the last trip I made in that vehicle.

As late spring approached, the search for teaching jobs became a focal point. While working at Elite Courier, both

Spiritual Seeds (Part 3)

Deb and I, through her Dad (who was a high school math teacher), were able to secure summer school teaching positions at her Dad's high school (R.S. McLaughlin). I got hired to teach biology, and Deb got hired to teach math. When the time came, I resigned from Elite Courier and Deb resigned from her temporary position at Homecare to begin lesson planning for upcoming summer classes. It was a lot of work! I was excited yet nervous about embarking on this new adventure, but the summer went well. It provided the opportunity to apply what we had learned at teacher's college not so long ago.

During our time at R.S. McLaughlin, we continued to apply for full-time teaching positions for the upcoming fall. As a result, Roger Lappin, the Principal of Duffin's Bay Public School, located in Ajax, Ontario, paid me a visit. He interviewed me for a grade seven and eight teaching position that had opened up at his school, and I got the job! Deb had also been granted an interview at a private school, called Trafalgar Castle, in Whitby, Ontario, and was offered a job teaching high school. Things were looking up! We were excited about starting into full-time teaching careers so soon after graduating from Teacher's College.

Not long after securing employment for the fall, we were able to find an apartment located on Taunton Road not far from my Mom and Dad's place, and moved in. It was a second-floor apartment, not huge by any means, but adequate for our family at the time. As the summer ticked along, not only was my mind beginning to focus more on getting ready for the coming fall, it was also alert to Deb's pregnancy. While she was teaching at R.S. McLaughlin, Deb began to go into labour. Off to the hospital we rushed, and as we parked the car in the above-ground parkade, her water broke just as she stepped out of the vehicle! Fortunately, we were not far from the front doors and made it there on time for her to hop onto a stretcher, get admitted, and then settle into a room. Not long after that, I witnessed the birth of our only son, John William Patrick Carr. It was July 19, 1984.

We were not able to access any benefits, such as maternity leave, at that time as we had not yet begun our first year of full-time teaching with the school division (Durham Board of Education). Consequently, once late August rolled around and the classroom beckoned us, Patrick and Julianna were placed in the hands of people we trusted to look after them while we were at work. We were always very fortunate to have those people around to help us out, which included family. I am not sure how we would have managed otherwise financially.

I worked at Duffin's Bay Public School for five years and had the privilege of working with and for many wonderful people. One incident, I recall, involved our school secretary. I was showing my class a film and was feeling very much under the weather that day. Once I had explained to the class what we were going to watch and why, I started the film, using an old reel-to-reel projector, and then nestled myself on the back counter still wearing my winter jacket. It was not long into the movie when Rita, our secretary, entered my classroom, came directly over to where I was seated on the counter and told me that my face looked yellow! I did not have a mirror handy, so I took her word for it and she left the room. She returned shortly after with a cup of hot chocolate and said with a serious tone, "This job will always be here. You might

Spiritual Seeds (Part 3)

not." In her concern, she was encouraging me to go home, see a doctor, and get some rest. I heeded her advice and thankfully so. I had pneumonia for the second time, but this time my left lung was half full of fluid! I was back to work five weeks later, weighing in at a hefty one hundred twenty-three pounds; I had lost at least twenty pounds! If it were not for Rita, my situation could have been much more dire indeed.

Our busy life, balancing home responsibilities, raising and providing for our family, and preparing and marking for classes, was taking its toll physically—and I was oblivious to it, until now. During my days of recovery, which included bouts of night sweats, taking horse pills, feeling short of breath, etc., I had time to think about life in general, and my thoughts and emotions were drawn to God. I remember writing a letter to Mom and Dad expressing how blessed I was to have them both as parents, and that I thanked God for them. In retrospect, even though I knew about God, Jesus, His birth, why He came to earth, and so on, I was still blind to the fact that I lacked a personal relationship with Him. I believe that God used this pneumonia situation to slow me down, take my focus off work, etc., and take stock of my relationship (and lack thereof) with Him. In other words, He was telling me to get my head out of the thorns—reminiscent of Matthew 13:22. I was still a religious moralist and lost, but God was still working on me.

My vice-principal at the school was John Ladd, a person who seemed to possess a quiet faith. He was an older man and a hoot to work with, but what stuck out in my mind was that he would, during morning announcements, humbly and faithfully recite the Lord's Prayer. He also demonstrated his graciousness when, during a Remembrance Day assembly, in front of a whole gymnasium full of students, their families, and relatives, he called up each class to lay a wreath at the cross they had set up on the stage. When it came time for me to send a student up to lay our wreath on behalf of our class, my jaw dropped—I had no wreath! I was the only teacher who had forgotten to prepare one. It was rather embarrassing for me and John, but he covered it well. He could have, and rightly so, tore a strip off me for putting him, myself, and my class in that position, like other administrators might have, but he did not. I learned very quickly to check my staff mailbox for notifications regularly after that! His tempered response spoke volumes to me. His demonstration of grace was reflective of that shown to Gary and me by our store manager and the big wig from Toronto, when they caught us playing hockey on the loading docks at Hudson's Bay.

His second co-administrator, and my second principal, by the name of Bill Waldron, was a godly man; the two of them worked very well together. I remember one time when Bill gave me a ride home from work. We drove on a route that took us past the Baptist Training Centre, which he pointed out to me and was familiar with, located somewhere between Oshawa and Ajax. Bill was never loud or pushy with his faith, but you knew he was a man of integrity and was serious about his faith and his responsibilities as lead principal of the school.

I recall one time, during the tenure of my first principal Roger Lappin, when a teacher had been recently hired who previously taught at a Christian school. The idea of a Christian School was somewhat new to me, so I was

Spiritual Seeds (Part 3)

curious what this new staff member was like and how she would fit in. Based on the times I talked with and observed her in the staff room, she seemed like a very nice lady. She seemed like any other teacher, but there was something different about her, not in a bad way, but there was just something different that I could not put my finger on. Sadly, there were some other staff members who worked on the same, or close to the same, wing of the school this teacher worked on. They were very critical of her behind her back and were uninhibited in how they expressed their opinion of her, through action and word, to the point I observed her in tears one day. I am not sure of the reasons for their attack on her, but she eventually resigned and returned to teach at the Christian School she left previously.

"What was it," I thought, "that made her come to our school in the first place, and what was it that the Christian school offered that made her want to return to it? Did she see it as a refuge and safe place? What was it that made it a form of refuge and a place of safety, other than familiarity? Was there a difference in the way people treated each other there? Was the work environment different there because it was a Christian school?"

The incident at our school, regarding this teacher, was certainly an example of how people can mistreat and disrespect each other even in places where professionals, who have been trained and taught to work with people, work. "How did I treat people, and what attitudes did I choose to hang on to regarding people who might differ from me? How might I handle such a situation if I was working with this same teacher?" I did not want to follow those colleagues' example, who drove this teacher to tears, but something inside told me that, because I am human, I was no different than those teachers and was capable of the same behaviour even though I tried to be a good person.

Not long after we had moved into our apartment, Deb and I went church shopping. We were curious about some of the other churches in and around our community and settled on trying out a Free Methodist Church in Whitby, Ontario. The people, including the pastor and his wife, were friendly and welcoming, so much so, that we decided to make it our church home; I also offered my services and joined the church cleaning crew. I remember one afternoon while vacuuming the sanctuary, Fred Gordon (the pastor) came in to say hello. I decided to take a quick break, which turned into more of a visit than a brief chat. Fred shared a little bit of his background and journey of how he came to faith in Christ and how he got into the ministry, which led to me opening up a bit about myself. During our discussion, Fred, I believe, must have sensed that I was not a true believer, though he did not say so, and gave me a Bible as well as a workbook entitled, *Life in Christ*. I was quite appreciative of his generosity and did make the effort to work through the questions and reflection sections of that workbook, in conjunction with my Bible. While spending time studying, I still felt that I was a Christian, that I was doing those things that were pleasing in God's sight and made me acceptable to Him, yet some of the material presented was new and challenging.

While teaching at Duffin's Bay Public School, I met a teacher who was filling in for our music teacher who happened to be sick that day. It turned out that this woman and her husband attended the same Free Methodist Church we were frequenting! While at church one Sunday,

Spiritual Seeds (Part 3)

they invited us over to their place for lunch after the service. We readily accepted and had a very welcoming visit with them. During our visit, the husband, whose name escapes my mind, described a moose hunting adventure in Northern Ontario that he had been part of the previous season, and how he was in the process of planning for the upcoming season. This perked my interest to the point that I began thinking of the possibilities for myself.

Another couple from Oshawa, who we met at church, was Richard and Rita Razcowski. We seemed to connect quickly and spent additional time with them outside of church as well. Like any other week, Sunday came and we headed off to church. As usual, people were gathering in the foyer outside the sanctuary to visit and chat before the service. When the people began to file into the sanctuary, Richard and I were still chatting and were left alone in the foyer. I remember mentioning to him about our visit with the couple whose husband was a moose hunter, and telling him how much I would love to go up north and hunt moose. As he nodded his head in approval, we proceeded into the service; Fred Gordon, our pastor, had been at the front of the sanctuary all along and was nowhere near the foyer at the time. I settled in on the pew with Deb and the kids and the hymns began, followed by the day's sermon.

As the sermon drew to a close, as was his custom, Fred gave an altar call, and it went like this: "Now is the time to give your heart to Jesus. Don't worry about hunting moose somewhere up North!" Fred could not possibly have heard me say that nor could anyone have mentioned it to him beforehand! That altar call caused me to take notice, but only temporarily, as I tucked that incident away. In hindsight, I believe that altar call was directed at me, that God was clearly speaking to me and trying to get my attention, in a rather direct way, but it did not sink in. I probably wrote it off as coincidence.

There was a woman who lived on the upper floor of our apartment who we came to know just by living in the same building. We were invited to her apartment one evening for a visit. Her name escapes me, but I remember that she had one or two children, no husband at home, and that she attended a Pentecostal church (a denomination I did not know much about). She explained that her husband had left her and the kids to pursue a relationship with another woman. We visited for a while and just before we were getting ready to leave, she asked if we could pray with her about her situation. We agreed and proceeded to do so. While praying, I could feel the fervency of her prayers and then it came around to my turn. I prayed as I had learned, or knew how to, at the end of which the woman commented on how she appreciated the way I prayed. I do not know what it was about my prayer that touched her, but somehow God must have used it. In hindsight, God was also teaching me that He desired me, and everyone, to come and talk with Him. He was showing me that He was not some impersonal, distant entity, but a real person who could be approached without fear, because of His love for His Creation. He desired a personal relationship with people, and He cared for our friend's concerns and burdens as He did mine. These were lessons that would become real for me in the not-too-distant future.

I met another couple who also lived on the upper floor of the apartment. The husband was an electronics

Spiritual Seeds (Part 3)

repairman, and his wife, who was Portuguese and loved cooking fish, was a stay-at-home Mom. They were a fun-loving couple who were always up for a chat. I remember one time I went to their apartment to borrow something and while there, I noticed a nicely framed diploma. Alongside it in the same folder, was a picture of the husband with some other men pulling a fishing net in from the water. I enquired about it and he told me that he had gone to Bible school; the picture was a visual of how, as a believer, he was a fisher of men (Matthew 4:19). I was intrigued. We chatted a bit more and then I had to return home to our apartment to attend to things. That image, and what it represented, stayed in my mind, though I did not fully understand the weight of it at the time.

One evening, while at our apartment, our son Patrick woke up not long after we had tucked him in for the night. He was about three or four years old, and woke up screaming in fear. I remember Deb and I rushing into his and Julianna's room trying to calm and console him as he looked around the room toward the ceiling with terror in his eyes. He was not hallucinating, was coherent, and was not in a sleep state; he was wide awake. As I sat with him, it was evident he was watching something, something scary, moving around the room, though I could not see anything. I went into protection mode, wanting to lash out at whatever was there, but there was nothing, at least not to my eyes. Eventually, Patrick calmed down, and we were able to get him back to sleep.

We never had an incident like that again, although Patrick did have occasional bouts of night terrors and sleepwalking some time after. In hindsight, I truly believe that was the first time I had ever witnessed an encounter, which appeared to be with the spiritual realm, and that Patrick genuinely saw something, though he could not put what he saw into words. It showed me that yes, there was indeed life beyond what I could see.

Around the same period, recollections of me being in my cousin Peter's basement leafing through magazines, so many years previous, kept coming to mind—particularly the image related to the Tribulation. For some time, with anxiety and fear, I would either wake up at night or in the middle of the day and start pleading with God to not leave me behind. By this point in my life, I had accumulated enough information, through others and written material, that I had some understanding of what was involved with this coming Biblical event, albeit that knowledge was still rudimentary. I remember those earnest and urgent pleadings like it was yesterday, and they recurred for about five years—pleadings that haunted me until I was thirty-two years old.

June 18, 1987 was a day of celebration as Deb gave birth to our third child (our second daughter), Caitlin Marie Carr. I remember travelling to St. Catherines after Caitlin was only a few months old, to introduce her to Deb's relatives. While there, we went to church with them, after which we spent some time showing off our new daughter to friends of the family. One couple had a young boy, probably about ten years old, who had Down Syndrome. With the assurance of this boy's parents, we carefully and cautiously placed our young daughter in his arms for him to hold. Not long after that Caitlin cried, spooking the boy who, in fear, dropped her right onto the concrete sidewalk!

We jumped into action, and with this boy's parents apologizing profusely, we rushed Caitlin off to the hos-

Spiritual Seeds (Part 3)

pital fearing the worst. Deb and Caitlin went on ahead with one set of relatives while Julianna, Patrick, and I followed with another set. I remember how hard we prayed together in the back seat of that car, that God would please not allow there to have been any injury. I felt utterly helpless and needed God's intervention. God did grant those prayers, and Caitlin came through without injury, particularly no head or brain injury. It was another lesson in throwing my cares and worries upon God, because He cared about what was going on and about what we were going through (1 Peter 5:7).

Caitlin's birth also prompted us to begin looking for a bigger place to live, as we were beginning to outgrow the small apartment we were occupying at the time. This was a new and exciting venture—stepping out looking to buy our very first house. While in the process, we became aware through an advertisement poster, that there was a new housing development taking place about twenty minutes east of Oshawa in a smaller community called Port Hope. Out of interest, we headed east to look at the potential dwellings they were constructing. While perusing the structures, our eyes caught a two-story, three-bedroom, two-bathroom house with an attached garage and a small backyard. It looked perfect for us, so we decided to fill out the appropriate paperwork and applied for a mortgage at the local bank. It did not take long for the application to be approved, and we became the proud owners of our first house for the price of $89,000!

Moving day came, and though we knew we would miss the people we had gotten to know in our community of Oshawa, our sights were set on moving into our brand-new home. The move was completed in stages. In short order we eventually got everything where it needed to be. Our new neighbourhood was still in the development stages, so there were not many homes in our area at that time. But that did not last for long. The builder responsible for the construction of these houses, including ours, was pumping them out, it seemed to me, in rather quick fashion. It was not long after we moved in, that we noticed the results of such construction practices. Not just us, but some of our neighbours noticed cracks in the basement walls which, for some, led to flooding. The staircase in our house was installed incorrectly, which led to a rebate of $5000 through house insurance, and the bay window displayed faulty installation. The first winter, our son Patrick's carpet had a light blanket of frost covering it, revealing that the insulation in the walls was substandard or absent—oh, the naiveté of a first-time homeowner!

After a short while, and after feeling somewhat settled, we began our search for a new church to attend. To start with, we thought we would check out the local Salvation Army in town. The church was in a small building and housed a small congregation; the people were very nice and welcoming. We could have easily continued to attend there, but we ended up attending an Anglican Church close to the house of the famous author Farley Mowat. This church (which was similar to what I was used to in Catholicism) was also welcoming and the people very friendly; consequently, we made it our church home. The minister and his family were warm people. I do remember having a hard time following the minister's sermons, however, as they were quite academic and over my head most times. The biggest benefit I believe I received was the fellowship with other attendees.

Spiritual Seeds (Part 3)

During our time attending this church, we met a couple by the name of Andre and Bonnie Cayer who had three children. Bonnie, we found out, was one of the children, back in the '70s, on the children's TV program, *The Mickey Mouse Club*. We became very good friends and realized they lived on the same street as we did! They were a great family, and fun to spend time with. Our neighbourhood in general, was a great environment for one to raise a young family. I remember Bonnie, though she attended the Anglican Church, saying she had some Evangelical roots, though she did not talk about it much.

I recall one incident at our house when I decided to do the laundry, which was in our basement. After removing the clothes from the washing machine, I placed them in a basket and had to run upstairs to get something. It was not long before I returned to my task and quickly dumped the basket of clothes into the dryer, closing the door, turning it on, and then heading back upstairs. As I was busying myself upstairs, I heard a strange noise coming from the basement. I stopped what I was doing to listen more carefully. As I listened, I could hear a distinctive, "Tha thump, meow; Tha thump, meow; Tha thump, meow." I hustled downstairs and realized the noise was coming from the dryer! I quickly opened the door and two cats, which we had become the proud owners of not long before, came diving out of the dryer and up the stairs! They must have buried themselves in the basket of clothes I dumped into the dryer! I must say, they had very soft and fluffy fur after that experience!

Teaching was going well for both Deb and me at our respective schools, but an opportunity came up for me to transfer to a new school that was closer to where we lived. I was granted the transfer and was hired to teach grades five and six at an inner-city school located in Oshawa. The school was called Mary Street Community School and I loved it there. It was a refreshing change from working with kids who, for the most part, came from very well-to-do families to working with students who were, in many cases, at the other end of the spectrum, and for the most part, lacked an entitlement attitude. It was a rougher teaching environment, but I felt quite at home, and the staff was second to none.

We had incredible unity as a staff and became quite close. At noon hours, in the spring and fall, me and another staff member named Lloyd, would go for a jog around the community. We had some great chats just about stuff. Nothing deep, but I remember one time when we were driving in his car, we were talking about something which led to him sharing about a speaker he had been listening to on a cassette tape. I am not sure what the speaker's name was, but Lloyd turned to me during our conversation and asked, "Are you religious?" I recall answering him by responding, "I am a Christian." We talked a little bit more and then moved on to another topic. If anything, that moment brought up the question, "Is there any difference between being religious and being a Christian? Are they one and the same or different?"— questions that I would not find the answer to for a few years to come.

I had the opportunity to teach night school at a local high school in Oshawa, after working my daytime teaching job at Mary Street. The motive for doing so was to earn some extra cash to help with paying bills and so on. My assignment was grade ten business math. Math was never my strong point in school, so I had a challenge ahead of me.

Spiritual Seeds (Part 3)

I dove in regardless. Once a week, I would head over to the high school right after work and begin preparing for class, which would start around 7:00 p.m. That gave me about two to three hours of prep time which I desperately needed, especially when it came to teaching algebra. I was very thankful that the answers to the student textbook questions were located in the back of the book!

After the class was adjourned, my usual routine was to take a leisurely drive home on Highway 2 to unwind from a very long and demanding day of work; I usually got home around 10:00 p.m. While driving, I would scan the radio stations to find something to listen to. While scanning one evening, I came across a radio station that aired a program called *The People's Gospel Hour*. I became quite intrigued by the program and what the radio preacher had to say. As a result, it became part of my routine each time I drove home from night school. There was nothing I can put my finger on that the preacher said that caught my attention; I just felt drawn while I listened to him teach from the Bible. This radio program was the only out-of-church Bible teaching I received, as I did not make Bible reading on my own, at the time, a regular part of my daily routine.

April 4, 1989 was another day for rejoicing as our fourth child, and third daughter, Emilie Suzanne Carr was born. Our expanding family and the construction issues with our house prompted us to look for greener pastures as far as living accommodations were concerned. We became aware of another housing development taking place just north of Cobourg, a community just northeast of our home at the time. The development was in a village called Baltimore. According to the advertisement, the homes they were building were beautiful and large enough to accommodate our growing family. As a result, we jumped in the car and headed north of Cobourg to check things out. When we arrived, it did not take long for us to decide on one of the houses that had recently been completed—a spacious, split-level bungalow, with an attached two-car garage, and a generous-sized yard. We made some inquiries and were able to negotiate a tentative agreement based on the sale of our present home. We were not long into the mortgage on our first home, with manageable payments, and were venturing into buying another home, if the first one sold, that was more expensive—$129,000 to be exact.

This new home brought with it higher payments, not only mortgage-wise but land tax-wise as well. Fortunately, it did not take long for our house in Port Hope to sell, at a higher price than what we'd anticipated, and we began preparing to move to our new abode. I remember the moving date was in the dead of winter, and it was chilly!

Baltimore was a beautiful community with a small-town feel. Our house was located right across from the community sports complex. It had spacious sports fields behind it that provided a great place to take our dog, Angel, who we inherited from Deb's Dad and Stepmother, for morning walks before work. I fondly remember one warm March day, during the school March break, taking Julianna and Patrick across to the sports complex parking lot and spending a good portion of the afternoon teaching them how to ride their bikes. It was a great place for families, as these amenities were so close.

I always looked forward to the regular trip to the local post office, which was in an older building not far from

Spiritual Seeds (Part 3)

our house, because it felt a little bit like going back in time. Though the housing development where we lived was modern and new, the atmosphere of the community was somewhat old-time country and I loved it. Despite all of that, however, there were times when I had bouts of wanting to pack everything up and take my family up north somewhere away from the hustle and bustle of our very busy life. My restlessness, and my desire to fill the emptiness I felt inside of me, drove those thoughts, though I had no idea what I was searching for.

On workdays, Deb would take Julianna and Patrick to school and I would take Caitlin and Emilie to the babysitters on my way to work in Oshawa. One morning, while driving the kids to the babysitters in south-end Oshawa, near the General Motors (GM) south plant, I came to a stop to wait for a vehicle in the opposing lane to pass before turning left onto the street where the babysitter's house was. As I stopped, I glanced in my rear-view mirror in time to see a vehicle, which had just left the GM plant, accelerate, without noticing my brake lights, toward the back end of my vehicle. I braced and then, Crash! I remember the impact caused the front bench seat of the car, where Caitlin and I were, to collapse backward onto Emilie, who was in the back seat buckled into her infant car seat. Her car seat prevented her legs from injury.

The force of the impact pushed our vehicle into the opposing lane, which fortunately had no traffic, and into the opposing curb, coming to a halt. I quickly checked on the kids. Caitlin bit her finger, which she must have had in her mouth on impact, and Emilie was unscathed, but crying. Other than that, there were no injuries to me or the girls. I could not open the car door, so I had to kick it open and then quickly retrieve the kids and take them to the sitters from where I could call the police. As I grabbed the girls, I glanced back at the driver who hit us and saw that he had a cut on his head and was semi-conscious. Before I checked on him, I needed to get the girls to safety and then return to the scene; all I could smell was gas.

By the time I got to the sitters and made the call, emergency crews were already at the scene—police, fire, and ambulance. Some other onlookers must have made the call before I was able to. When I returned, I could see that the gas tank, which I had just filled, had ruptured on impact. I found out later that the fire crew was scratching their heads as to why the gas did not erupt into flames or explode; there was no question in my mind that a bigger hand had a say in this. I gave my statement to a police officer, who then graciously gave me a lift to work. Upon arriving at work, the staff was surprised to see me as news of the accident was already on the radio. From their reaction to the radio report, it seemed they were not sure whether or not I and the girls had survived the accident; they thought we might have died. I called Deb at work to let her know what had happened and to assure her that we were all okay. She was obviously shaken and when she asked if she could leave to be with her family, her administrator said, "No!" Deb was not impressed! She had no choice but to stay at work. It never really sank in just how serious and potentially deadly that accident could have been—until later. It was a lesson in the brevity and fragility of life.

Shortly after we purchased the house in Baltimore, I transferred from Mary Street Community School in Oshawa to Thomas Gillbard School in Cobourg, just

Spiritual Seeds (Part 3)

twenty minutes from home! At the same time, Deb secured a teaching job at another school in Cobourg as well, which made gas expenditure and time on the road much more manageable. The teaching environment at Gillbard was very similar to Mary Street in that it was an inner-city school, which brought with it some of the same familiar social issues I experienced while working in Oshawa. Staff dynamics were also similar in their comradery.

Working at Gillbard was a lot of fun and I genuinely looked forward to being involved at the school each day. In my first year there, I worked under the leadership of a man by the name of Bruce Steele, with whom I became very good friends, and referred to him as "Iron Man." I taught a grade seven and eight class, and it was Bruce's approach that provided the opportunity to try new things and pursue activities, within reason, that were enjoyable for staff and students. Consequently, I spent many hours coaching basketball, running an outdoor education club, coaching the Gillbard tug-of-war team, and so on. It was a place where, like Mary Street, the administration, community, and students appreciated the time and effort put in to make school meaningful and enjoyable.

I remember an awards assembly toward the end of my first year. We gathered in the gym, and each teacher had the opportunity to get up and say a few words. When it came to my turn, I reminisced about the fun experiences I had with my class throughout the year, particularly on our outdoor education trip weekend to Ganaraska Forest. Even today I recall with fondness, the bonding that occurred through that event. After the assembly concluded, one of the relatives of the students came up to me and said, in genuineness, that he thought I sounded more like a vicar (a member of the clergy) than a teacher when I spoke. I do not know what it was I said, or how I said it that prompted him to say that, but that comment, being unexpected, stuck in the back of my mind.

One incident I recall, involved a grade five student who was having an outburst after school in one of the classrooms. The school custodian and I were in the vicinity, so we responded to help the classroom teacher. When we arrived, this student was out of control to the point that he had to be restrained on the floor or he was going to hurt someone. I remember the custodian, who was about two hundred pounds, laying on this boy's legs to keep him from kicking. I was at the other end trying to restrain his arms so he could not hit anyone. I turned to look and see how John, the custodian, was doing and I could not believe my eyes! Here was John, a two-hundred-pound man, laying on a grade five student's legs, a student who was much smaller in stature, and the boy was bouncing John up and down like a rag doll just by bending his legs! I could not believe what I was seeing! The boy was doing this with no effort at all! This was impossible! I turned to look at the boy's face and I remember seeing his eyes wide open with an eerie glaze. I firmly said to the boy, as I battled to keep his arms under control, "You're going to lose." Shortly after that, I saw the glaze start to dissipate, his eyes return to normal, and his body relax. It was a dark experience, evil-like, and one that I wondered after if something else was involved with this boy's ability to physically do what I saw him do. That incident weighed on my mind for some time after.

Moving to Baltimore precipitated looking for a new church home. Having attended an Anglican Church while

Spiritual Seeds (Part 3)

in Port Hope made it natural to seek out an Anglican Church to attend in Cobourg, which we did. We settled on making St. Peter's Church, an ornate, huge cathedral, our place of worship. Though it was big, and the congregation large, the people, including the ministers, were very welcoming. It was the first church that I ever desired to volunteer to help with a Sunday School class. There was no interview or vetting process beforehand, like I observed with Rob back in London, Ontario, to tell of my faith journey or how I came to Christ; it seemed to be assumed that I was a Christian, which was fine with me because I thought I was. Consequently, I was welcomed into the class. It was also the first time I ever played my guitar in front of anyone. I remember teaching the class, "Amazing Grace," a hymn that resonated with me, but I did not, at that time, realize the depth and real meaning of the words.

One Sunday, which happened to be around Halloween, the children's Sunday School classes hosted a costume day. I remember standing on the church balcony after class, watching the costumed students walk down the center aisle of the church parading their costumes. As I watched, I noticed a young student dressed in a devil costume. It struck me as peculiar to see a costume, innocently worn by the boy, which portrayed a character that was so anti-God openly displayed and seen as acceptable and cute in a place such as a church. It created a bit of a paradox in my mind, though I kept it to myself.

We missed our friends Richard and Rita Rascowski from Oshawa, as they did us, so they began looking for an opportunity to move closer so we could more easily see each other. Not long after we moved, an opportunity did present itself for them to buy a house in Cobourg—an opportunity which they availed themselves of to our hearty approval. I found out later that sometime before our and their move to the area, Richard had asked the pastor of Lakeshore Free Methodist Church in Cobourg to drop by to say hello. He called ahead and we arranged a time that worked for all of us.

The day came and the pastor, Herb Van Essen, presented himself at our door and we invited him in. We had a good visit around the kitchen table, after which Herb concluded by inviting us to consider coming to his church. We thanked him for the visit and the invitation and said we would give it some serious thought. We did think it through and decided we would accept Herb's invitation. In hindsight, I believe my friend Richard, who was involved with evangelistic work overseas during his time off from work, sensed that I was not what the Bible refers to as a born-again believer, though he never verbalized this to me, and consequently encouraged Herb to contact us.

Lakeshore Free Methodist Church was a small congregation of about fifty people who were very warm, welcoming, supportive, and encouraging. They made us feel very much at home among them. The kids enjoyed attending Sunday School as Deb did teaching it. We all made some very good friends while there. The preaching was Bible-based and not delivered in such a way that it could not be understood by a person without formal Bible training. It was a good learning environment, as was our time at Whitby Free Methodist Church.

It was around this time that Deb and I began to run into financial challenges. With student loans, increased mortgage and land tax payments, and other miscellaneous expenditures, we were forced to declare bankruptcy. In

Spiritual Seeds (Part 3)

hindsight, we should have stayed in the house we had in Port Hope, which was smaller and would have been adequate. There, things were more manageable financially, but we moved ahead too quickly and made some unwise financial decisions. We were now seeing the fruit of that; despite these circumstances, however, God would use them for our benefit.

As a result of declaring bankruptcy, our house in Baltimore went on the market for quick sale to help pay off the balance of the mortgage, which necessitated looking for another place to live. We also made effort to sell what we could not take with us to help with other costs involved with our move, such as our first and last months' rent on a rental property—a property which we had not yet secured. It was a tough decision, and we were sad that we had to do what we did, but if anyone must learn a lesson such as this, you only want to learn it once!

Our search for a rental property began in earnest. Through word of mouth, we were made aware of an older home that was available for rent southeast of us along Highway 2 in a small village named Grafton. We were provided with a contact name and number and arranged a time that we could go and look at the house. Within a day or two, we headed to Grafton armed with a few questions about the property. Upon arrival, we were surprised to see how big the house was! In our discussion with our contact, who happened to be the person managing the property, we found out that it was the former Anglican Church Manse, or Rectory, for the Anglican Church which happened to be right across the highway.

The house was a century home built sometime in the early 1900s with an ornate entryway, a beautiful wooden stairway leading to the second floor, a study, four bedrooms, a living room, a sitting room, a huge storage room, and a country-sized kitchen with a walkout deck! The yard was quite large with mature trees, including blackberry and chestnut trees, a garage, an ample-sized vegetable garden, and a creek running through the lower part of the backyard. The house was also right across from the skating rink and ball diamond! This place was well beyond what we could ever have asked for or imagined! What we had to give up was replaced by something better. It was a no-brainer. We signed on the dotted line and arranged a move-in date. In retrospect, it was an illustration of a person giving up their present way of living (a life of sin) and exchanging it for the life Christ gives through faith in Him—a life that is well beyond what we could ask for or imagine.

Grafton was a neat little place nestled in the country outside of city limits. It had the basic amenities such as a small convenience store, a Co-op Agro store, three churches (Catholic, Anglican, and United), a gas station with repair bays, and an elementary school. Grafton was also only a short bike ride from Lake Ontario, which allowed some occasional shore fishing, within season of course.

I have many good memories of our time in Grafton. Many kilometers were put on the pedal bikes with the kids, going to the Lakeshore to look for fossils on the stone beach or just for the fun of riding. During the winter, after a big snowfall, we made snow angels in the side yard and slipped in the odd snowball fight.

I remember one incident when I invited the basketball team I coached at Gillbard, for an end-of-the-year barbecue. In our kitchen, behind the washer and dryer and along the back wall were the pipes that carried wash water from the washer to the underground septic tank in the backyard. These pipes ran vertically above the floor against the wall into which the discharge hose from the washer would fit. Someone was in the washroom upstairs at the time and flushed the toilet. As we were all settling around the table ready to dig into the food, the sewage pipe from the toilet became plugged, causing a back-up, forcing the sewage up the washer drainpipe like a geyser and onto the kitchen floor right beside the table where everyone was seated. And, you guessed it, everything came up from those pipes. Believe me, it did not smell like roses! It was truly gross, but everyone split a gut laughing before we kicked into gear and started emergency clean-up. It was a memory-maker!

Living in the country also brought with it the romantic idea of having additional animals to care for; consequently, we caved to the idea of adding to our pet collection. As a result, we ended up with five cats, two dogs, and three rabbits—our own pet farm! Our pets came indoors as well and were very much part of the family. In retrospect however, as much as I love pets, I would now opt out and greatly limit bringing animals indoors! They were lots of fun, but much work at times and needed to be constantly watched outdoors due to our proximity to the highway, although it was not very heavily travelled. Despite our best efforts, our cat population decreased through attrition as they were not very wise and wary of the road. As a result, the east side of our yard, along the hedges, became somewhat of a pet cemetery.

Amid all the changes that had happened regarding our living circumstances, Deb's and my teaching jobs remained constant and were progressing well. Deb taught a grade seven and eight class at her school, Grant Sine Public School, and was also involved in coaching the school basketball team. Several times, her team and mine would get together to play exhibition games to help develop each of our player's skills. One of her proteges, a forward by the name of Peter Smith, was a terrific and talented basketball player and was a key component to her team. Through her coaching and teaching, Deb befriended Peter's mother Linda, who was a single Mom, who also had a friend by the name of Tim. Unbeknownst to me, these two people were to play a pivotal role in God's plan to bring me to Himself.

Lakeshore Pentecostal Camp

*Many are the plans in a man's heart,
but it is the Lord's purpose that prevails.*
(PROVERBS 19:21)

With a roof carrier jammed to roof-denting capacity, a car interior inhabited by two adults, four kids, a full-grown dog, and numerous bags of luggage, we made a last-minute check before heading off for that long-awaited dream vacation to head west. With visions of majestic mountains, harvest-moon evenings, and fields of golden wheat embossed in my mind from recently read travel magazines, we set out on our quest to the sound of popular tunes belting from the car radio, the slobbery panting of our dog, and the inevitable question, "Are we there yet?"

It was July 1992, and it was hot and humid! Everyone on board adjusted quite well to the heat and lack of air conditioning in the old Dodge Diplomat, as we looked forward to the adventure that awaited us down the highway. We encountered many points of interest along the way, but one of the biggest we had as a family, was touring through the Calgary Zoo. This place was enormous and a great place to spend most of the afternoon. The variety and quality of the exhibits were exceptional. The kids particularly enjoyed the dinosaur display section.

Due to the fact we had time restraints, we were unable to push through to British Columbia, but that was okay because there were lots of places to stop off at and see on our way back to Ontario. One place was Buffalo Pound Provincial Park, located northeast of Moose Jaw, Saskatchewan. Upon arrival, we were not sure if any campsites were available, but fortunately we were able to secure a spacious camping spot where we could comfortably set up camp and stay for a night or two.

Buffalo Pound Park was a beautiful place. It was situated along the banks of Buffalo Pound Lake, a popular boating and fishing lake for area residents and campers. It also offered playgrounds for kids, a mini-golf course, picnic areas, a swimming pool, a trout pond, a look-out spot to watch bison, and a convenience store. There were lots of things to occupy people and it was a great place to spend as a family. I remember one time when I went into the convenience store to buy something. While there, my eye caught a display containing a variety of books for purchase. Out of curiosity, I walked over to peruse what was there. Nestled among the many titles that were offered, I noticed a small book entitled *My Utmost for His Highest* by Oswald Chambers. I had never heard of this title or author before. After skimming the cover and contents, I realized it was a Christian devotional divided into daily inspirational readings for each day of the year. As I stood there, I felt compelled to buy it, and so I did. In the evenings, after the kids were settled into bed and things were quiet around the campsite, I would take some time to read out of this little book. It was a little hard to follow, as it was written in an old English style, but despite that, I sensed a kind of contentment just having the book in my possession.

The day came when it was time to load up and get ready for the trip home. I remember that, before pulling up stakes and hitting the road, we took one last walk around the park just to soak up the stillness and quietness of the surroundings. As we walked down to the lakeshore, I asked a person sitting at one of the picnic tables if they would take a picture of us with the lake in the background, for memory-making purposes, and they obliged. As we headed back to the car, I recall either mentioning to Deb or praying to God how much I would like for us to come back to Saskatchewan to live. Little did I know how those words would be fulfilled in a way I could never have imagined.

As much as we would have liked to stay, we did look forward to getting home and returning to the familiar sights and sounds of Grafton, Ontario, which also happened to be the hometown of the gentleman who played the role of the friendly giant on the *Friendly Giant* children's show—one that I watched as a young kid. We did our best to soak up the sights as best we could as we travelled home, knowing it would not be long before our time would be absorbed by school.

We arrived home in early August and the time drew near for us to begin getting things ready for the new crop of young grade seven and eight minds that would spill over into our classrooms in the rapidly approaching fall. Another school year had almost arrived and had somehow snuck up on me faster than I anticipated, and with that, the jitter-producing unknowns: "What will my students be like? Will my classes bring with them some serious discipline issues? What additional responsibilities will I be asked to take on in addition to an already busy academic schedule?" and so on. As much as I enjoyed teaching, I never looked forward to the pressures that came with every new school year in the form of increased hustle and bustle, the ever-present balance of work and family responsibilities, the hours spent on lesson planning and marking, and returning to a rigid schedule, although a certain amount of structure was always good.

It was around this time, shortly after arriving back home, and in the midst of frantic preparation for the fall, that Linda Smith and her friend Tim, who had become good friends of ours, showed up on the doorstep of our home unannounced to invite us to an outdoor event. I was a bit cautious at first because I realized that this event was connected with the Pentecostal Church, a denomination I remember the lady from the apartment we lived in Oshawa was part of, and one that I now knew Linda was affiliated with. The event they were inviting us to was a camp meeting (something I had never experienced), or service, to be held about fifteen minutes west of our place. My friend, Colin Woolmer, who was a former boyfriend of my sister Nancy, arrived earlier that afternoon for an impromptu visit, so the invitation was also extended to him. Though I respected and trusted Linda and Tim, I began fumbling over my words to come up with any believable excuse so I could back out of going, due to my discomfort over the whole thing, even speaking for Colin, saying that he might find it uncomfortable. As a result of that, I reasoned, it would be more considerate if I were to stay at the house with him rather than place him in that kind of situation.

Without missing a beat, Colin spoke up and said he would like to go and check out the music! Consequently, my cover was blown, and I reluctantly found myself heading out the door on my way to the church service early that evening! "Why did I need to go? Should people who do not attend church be the ones invited to these things, and not people who already go to church?" I asked myself. "After all, I was a regular church attendee. We, as a family, had been attending the local Free Methodist Church and I considered myself already part of the flock. I did not need to go to something that I already felt I had a handle on. I knew about God, Jesus, and the Bible. I even knew a little about something called the Rapture, the Tribulation, end times, and other stuff." The thought of going to this unfamiliar outdoor service, at an unknown location, made me wiggle.

I continued to ask myself: "Who was going to be there in attendance? Will I know anybody? Who was the speaker and what was he going to speaking about?" It felt downright uncomfortable to me to walk into something that might take me outside of and challenge my understanding of what church meant and was, of who God was, of who Jesus was, and what it meant to be a Christian. It also made me nervous about the possibility that I might be challenged in my lifestyle, not that I felt I was living a bad life. I felt I was okay. I was considered a nice guy and got along well with most people. I tried to do the right things in my dealings with others, and I had a successful teaching career underway. I had four healthy children and a wife and was doing much better financially. "Why did I need to go? Why could I not just stay at home, hang out with Colin, or find some other reason, and those who wanted to go could go?" I was dragging my heels all the way!

It was a beautiful, warm evening when we headed west from Grafton, travelling along Highway 2. After about fifteen minutes, I turned left, following Linda and Tim, onto a long, unfamiliar secondary road that led toward the shore of Lake Ontario. "Where were we going?" I had never been this way before. I looked for anything that would indicate where we were, and soon a sign came into sight saying "Lakeshore Pentecostal Camp." The nervousness and uncertainty began to build inside of me, but I kept driving. In the distance, I could see the shape of several large buildings and cottages, as well as vehicles coming and going from the campgrounds. From what I saw, it looked to be a busy place, set in a beautiful location overlooking the lake, but I was also wondering what I was in for. "Why was I feeling the way I was? Maybe Colin and I could hang out while everyone else went in to the service," I strategized. We turned off into a grassy parking area where several cars had already parked. As we got out of the vehicle, I noticed other vehicles following in behind us and filling up the parking area quite quickly. "This sure is attracting a lot of people," I thought to myself.

Once we met up with the others in our group, Colin, Tim, Linda, Deb, me, and the kids, with Linda directing, headed toward the Camp chapel. Given my past, my idea of church was that it was held in a traditional church building, not a storage-type looking building, with anywhere from fifty to one hundred and fifty attenders, and located somewhere in town, not somewhere off the beaten track. I was not expecting to see what I saw before me! There had to have been, what looked to me, at least six hundred people in attendance! People were happily greeting each other, some sitting, some searching for a seat, and others just socializing. I suggested to Deb that she and the kids go and find a seat with the rest of the group and I would be along shortly, while in my mind I intended to stand by the back entrance doors for an easy escape if things started feeling uncomfortable. The attendance continued to grow to the point that extra seating had to be set up outside of the main entrance and, as a result, I found myself surrounded. I still, however, would have space to slip away if the situation warranted it.

The service soon got started and by this time there seemed to be standing room only, with some live music followed by an introduction to the evening's speaker. His name was Rich Wilkerson, a well-known evangelist apparently, judging by the reaction of the people in the seats. I had heard of David Wilkerson, author of *The Cross and the Switchblade* who also was a well-known evangelist, but was not sure if they might be related. His talk that evening centered on end times—a topic that stirred up butterflies, fear, and anxiety within me and acted as the catalyst for the events that followed.

Previous to this evening, as I mentioned earlier, I had been plagued for about five years with a nightmarish fear of the end times, in particular the Tribulation. I would wake up in the night pleading with God to please not leave me behind to face the Tribulation and the horrors that were to unfold during this coming prophesized event.

As Rich Wilkerson continued his message, he began giving examples of how the world was moving toward the

Rapture and, inevitably, the Tribulation. That hit a raw nerve and was my cue. My strategy to hang out by the back entrance was put into play. I slinked away from the chapel and began to pace the campgrounds aimlessly and anxiously. The setting of Lakeshore Camp was beautiful and spacious, but it was not the scenery that was absorbing my very being at that moment! I was an emotional wreck, bawling my eyes out as I walked, pleading with God, and reaching out to Him for some assurance that He was not going to leave me behind during the Tribulation. I was unsure of where I stood concerning this. "Was God going to leave me behind? What about Deb and the kids? Why did I feel so empty inside, so unsure, so imprisoned by fear?" The feelings and thoughts going on inside of me were relentless! The physical feelings were intense, but it was, in reality, more than that. Though I did not recognize it as such at the time, there was a very real spiritual battle going on inside of me for my very soul.

I am not sure how long I had been pacing the campgrounds, but I am sure I covered a distance that would make any long-distance walker proud! Amid my struggle and painful yearning for reassurance and solace, I felt drawn back to the chapel—something that was not at the top of my list to do. "Why did I want to go back there? I left there because I was uneasy with and anxious about what was being talked about. Why would I want to walk back into that situation? Why would I feel that I should go back to the chapel—it just did not make sense!" Nonetheless, I felt compelled to go and found myself heading back in that direction, not knowing what was going to happen next.

In recent years, leading up to me returning to the entrance of the chapel, Deb and I had tossed around some ideas as to what we would like to do when, in the future, the day came to retire from teaching. Retirement was sometime in the distant future, but it was still kind of fun to dream a bit. One of the ideas that seemed to appeal to both of us, was to retire to a log cabin somewhere in northern Ontario. Due to our love for the north and the outdoors, it was a natural choice. We then toyed around with doing some preliminary exploration into what would be involved in planning out such an adventure.

I approached the back entrance of the chapel, anxiously stepped inside, and stood observing what was going on. I noticed people were riveted on every word Wilkerson had to say; not a sound could be heard except the commanding voice of the speaker, but what caught my attention was when he made the invitation to come forward to the altar. Keep in mind there were at least six hundred people in attendance and I had never met Rich Wilkerson in person, let alone heard of him before this evening. In his altar call, he said, "Now is the time to give your heart to Jesus. Do not worry about wanting to retire to a log cabin somewhere up north!!" My eyes froze on the evangelist. "Did I hear what I thought I heard?" There were at least six hundred people in that chapel. How could anyone, let alone the speaker, have known I was thinking of wanting to retire to a log cabin somewhere up north? "He could not be speaking to me!" I thought. This was the second time something like this had happened, the first being at Whitby Free Methodist Church a few years earlier! "He must have meant someone else," I reasoned. "This must be a coincidence." Or was it? I was meant to be there. Little did I know that God was not going to let me off the hook.

Searching

...If you seek Him, He will be found by you...
(1 CHRONICLES 28:9)

Watching several people slowly move out of their seats and into the aisles in response to the altar call did not do much to encourage me to follow. I was determined to stay planted at the rear entrance of the chapel and rooted myself there until the closing hymn of the service. In the meantime, I kept observing what was happening around me. As people were milling about, in response to the altar call, others were standing at their seats, while others held their hands raised. Some were sitting and some kneeling, and some quietly speaking to themselves in a strange language, which I later learned was "speaking in tongues." In all of this, with music gently playing in the background, there was an overwhelming sense of sincere worship and quiet reverence. I did not sense any phoniness; it was beautiful!

The whole building was filled with a warmth of stillness and peace; people were not in a hurry to leave to rush out to get to the parking area first, as one might see at the end of a hockey game at the local arena. I had never experienced this type of gathering before on such a scale; there was such joy and contentment in these people, yet I was in knots! "What made them different? What did they have that I did not?" I asked myself. I could not fully process all that was happening, but one question was at the forefront of my mind: "Was I going to be left behind during the Tribulation?" That question was still unanswered and occupied my very being. The evangelist's invitation, "Now is the time to give your heart to Jesus. Do not worry about wanting to retire to a log cabin somewhere up north," did catch me off guard, but because of my absorption with the question of my status in relation to the Tribulation, I was distracted. In response, I desired to leave as quickly as I could at the end of the service, letting this "coincidence" go right over my head. I was more concerned and focused on having my question answered, to the point that I was blind to what God was directly saying to and placing before me. In my mind, Jesus was real, but had I given my heart to Jesus? and what did it really mean?

People eventually began filing out of the chapel in larger numbers, some lagged around the altar, while others went into a back room to talk with one of the pastors who was on hand to assist anyone who needed it. I was not one of those, I thought. I was so in knots at the time. I was not in the frame of mind, nor did I know how to turn to anyone for help, but that would soon change.

I began to seek out where Deb and the kids were seated. We then met up with Tim and Linda; Colin had already left the service sometime earlier. We all exchanged

Searching

our opinions of what we thought of the service and the message given by the preacher. When it came to my turn, I did not know what to say, so I just echoed everyone else by saying it was a great service, that I got much out of it, and that Rich Wilkerson was a very good speaker. None of them had any idea of the turmoil that was twisting and turning inside of me; though it was hard, I was able to display a calm exterior. I was not in any state of being able to express what I was struggling with; the battle kept my focus turned inward. I was fearful of the horrific events that were to happen during the Tribulation and the uncertainty of whether I would be left behind; it was as though I was shackled to this anxiousness and fear without knowing how to deal with it. I was in this myself, so I thought, not knowing who to go to for consolation and trustworthy answers, and I was desperate for answers!

The pathways were now choked with people coming from the chapel, so we just dove into the "salmon run" and made our way to the grassy area where our vehicles were parked. There was not much opportunity to talk amongst ourselves on our way to the vehicles, but when we did finally get there, we thanked Tim and Linda for inviting us and mentioned that it would be nice to get together again soon. We hopped into our respective cars and began to make our way home. The evening was warm, with a clear sky, yet mental clouds impeded my concentration on what was going on around me. I was preoccupied with my thoughts; consequently, it was a relatively quiet ride. After leaving the camp service, writing off the altar call incident as "coincidence," unawares to me, the upcoming week was testimony that God's pursuit of me was not finished.

We arrived home, bundled up the kids, and walked through the front door to the usual greeting of our three dogs, five cats, and three rabbits. It was not long before we started yawning and headed for the comfort and security of our beds. After bedtime prayers and kisses goodnight, it was time to rest and reflect on the day. For me, this was just the beginning.

After falling asleep, I began dreaming. I dreamt that I was standing at the top of our wooden stairway looking down toward our front door. I had an eerie feeling come over me like we were in the midst of the Tribulation. Suddenly, there was banging and crashing. Someone or something was trying to break through the front door into the house! I knew by the relentless and aggressive sounds, that whoever or whatever, on the other side of that door, was intent at getting at us—for what reason I did not know. It was as though we were enemies to someone, something, or some ideal that these figures behind the door represented. With my heart hammering in my chest, I tried to run to get Deb and the kids to safety but could not. My feet were frozen where they were; the muscles in my legs became stiff from struggling to move. The banging and pounding on the door increased until suddenly, a hole was punched through, then another, and another. Crash! The door blew into hundreds of splinters as three armed, masked men hurried through the opening where the door once stood. I tried to hide but could not; I was in full view of these unknown trespassers. I had no way of escape! "What did they want? What about Deb and the kids? How was I to protect them and was I going to be able to protect them?" I was helpless!

Searching

As I stood there, I watched the men quickly look around the house. It was obvious they were not interested in stealing any material things, they were looking for us! As this was happening, it seemed that I was invisible to them. They did not even see me though I was totally in their line of sight. At times, it felt as though I was hovering above them. It felt weird!

When the screaming started, all I could think about was Deb and the kids. In fearful anticipation, I asked myself, "What is happening? Why can I not go to them? What is going on?" Then the gunshots! Oh, the gunshots and sickening, horrific knot in my gut. Though I did not see it happen, I knew my family was dead, murdered by these unknown assailants. My heart was racing, the sweat beading on my forehead. The pain and horror of the events I had just been witness to were more than I could bear.

If I had not been jolted out of my dream at that point, I felt that I might not have woken up ever again! I sure did not need a cup of coffee; that dream was all the caffeine I needed! "Why did I have that kind of dream?" I asked myself. "What was it I was to take from it?" I was terrified, and the fears and uncertainties of whether or not I was going to have to go through the Tribulation came back in full force. This was just a beginning to a week I will never forget, a week in which I believe God allowed me to go through my own personal tribulation.

The specific days of the week in which events took place are a blur because I was numb to everything and everyone around me it seemed. I had no appetite, could not eat even if I wanted to, or carry on a conversation for any length of time as I was so restless. I do not even remember talking with the kids all that week. I was so absorbed by what was going on inside of me mentally, emotionally, and physically. It was as though I was the only one within the circle of people I knew, going through what I was going through. I felt lost, but lost from what?

I could no longer hide from my family the fact I was having a significant struggle within—they could see it. I was a zombie! I cried during my waking hours and cried myself to sleep—if I slept. I was shackled with fear, pacing with no direction. I felt empty, yet powerfully drawn by and toward something. I was looking for answers, but to whom should I go? Who could I turn to?

The first name that came to mind was the pastor of the church we were presently attending, namely Lakeshore Free Methodist Church. During our time there, Herb, the pastor, and we became good friends, so I felt comfortable talking with him about the prevailing question circulating in my mind. I picked up the phone, in nervous anticipation, not knowing what answer he would give to the question, "Will I have to go through the Tribulation?" With a shaky hand, I pressed the receiver tightly to my ear. I dialed the number and listened intently to the ringing on the other end of the phone line. "Was he going to pick up the phone? When? Maybe I should hang up. Do I really want to hear what he might say?"

Not long after asking myself those questions, Herb answered, "Hello." "Hi, Herb! It is John calling. Can I ask you a question?" "Sure," Herb said. "What's up?" "Are we going to have to go through the Tribulation?" I asked nervously, bracing myself for his response. "The early Church fathers and Christians of Bible times went through some very trying times because of their faith. Why should we be any different?" he asked. "So, you are saying that we will

Searching

have to go through the Tribulation?" I questioned nervously. "Yes, I believe there is a good chance we will have to go through it, based on the experiences the Christians had during the early foundation of the Christian church." I let that sink in for a moment and then responded, "Thanks, Herb. I need to think through this a bit. I'll talk to you a bit later."

Herb and I ended our conversation, but there was a nagging within me that left me with a sense that what Herb had said about Christians having to go through the Tribulation, was not right. Though I respected Herb's input, something just did not sit right with me in the answer he gave. I do not know why, but the conviction was there. I was not trying to seek out people who would give me the answer I wanted to hear; I would have accepted Herb's answer if it was not for this nagging conviction something was wrong. I was on a determined mission to find the right answer to my question.

The preoccupation with whether I was going to have to go through the Tribulation consumed me. All my energy, time, and focus were invested in trying to seek someone out that would give me the right answer to this question that resonated in my very being. I felt like I was in a world of my own, a pilgrim on a desert journey searching for an oasis to quench my thirst for counsel and a solution to my dilemma. The nightmares; lack of appetite; fitful, sleepless nights; tears; and constant restlessness continued throughout the week. It seemed unending! I did not know who to turn to. I needed the key to release me from this prison of fear and uncertainty I found myself in.

I called my brother-in-law Jim who had, along with Kara and their kids, moved to the area, and asked if he would be willing to come over to our place and talk. I called Jim thinking that, because of his involvement in his church, he might be able to shed some light on my question. He willingly agreed. I remember us sitting on the front porch of the house and me asking the question about the Tribulation. I respected Jim's opinion and considered him a close brother-in-law, but I did not expect the answer he gave. In his sincerity to help, Jim seemed to convey the idea that the Tribulation was nothing to worry about, like it was not a real event. I do not remember his exact words, but I could feel the fear and anxiety leave me almost immediately upon hearing his words. I felt relieved.

A very short while after however, I rose out of my chair convicted that something just did not add up in what he said. I knew the Tribulation was a real event because it was laid out in Scripture. We walked to his vehicle and I said to him, "What about Noah? Did God not rescue him from the flood?" and "What about Lot? Did God not rescue him and his family from His judgment on Sodom and Gomorrah? Did God not pull them out before He poured out His wrath? Why would that not also apply to Christians—people who follow Him?" I did not feel that my question had been answered and the fear, uncertainty, and anxiety reappeared. "Who was I to turn to next?"

I had talked with my pastor and my brother-in-law, but nothing came out of that to satisfy my search, so I went back to my church roots; I contacted the local office of the village priest to set up an appointment to have a chat. "Did he have the answer?" I needed to settle this once and for all!

When the time came, I headed out the front door of our house and walked toward the Village's only Catholic Church, which was about a ten to fifteen-minute walk.

Searching

Along the way, my stress level was palpable; my mind was racing in anticipation and wonder as to what the priest would say as well as how I would verbalize what I was going through. Once I reached the church doors, I knocked and was greeted by, I think, the church secretary. I was then ushered into a relatively large room where the priest was seated at one end, looking out a window. He was an older gentleman, one that appeared to have been in the ministry for most of his adult life. I took a seat a distance away opposite him; it seemed quite formal and impersonal. The conversation was not long, as I was very focused, and asked the priest if we would have to go through the Tribulation. He answered that yes, we would have to. What struck me as unusual was he made no eye contact with me for the duration of my visit, nor did he offer any words of wisdom or comfort. I prodded him more, and then thanked him for his time and left.

Though my convictions suggested otherwise, I asked myself, "Was this really the way it was going to play out—that I would have to go through the Tribulation?" I could contain my composure no longer. No sooner had I gotten out the door of that church, I broke down and cried profusely as I walked home. Amid my emotional agony, I began hearing, in my heart and mind, the words, *Be still, and know that I am God, be still, and know that I am God* (Psalm 46:10) over and over. Along with that, I heard in my mind the words, "You have run to everyone else for answers, but you have not come to the One who knows" (1 Samuel 2:3; Ecclesiastes 8:7). These words gave me an unusual comfort mixed in with unsettled emotions and fear—an unusual mixture indeed. I did not know what to fully make of all this.

Our friends Linda and Tim had been invited over that evening for supper and Bible study; they had no idea how my day had unfolded before they came. I arrived home from my visit with the priest and, having pulled myself together before entering the house, it was not long before our company arrived.

It was August 14, 1992; I remember the weather being muggy but beautiful that evening. Though I was able to pull myself together, my gut was still in knots; I felt frantic inside, and I needed answers—NOW! I could not contain myself any longer with the façade that everything was okay. "Tim!" I said anxiously, as he and Linda were about to walk through our front door. "Can we go for a walk? I need to talk to you." Tim responded, "Sure." I quickly walked out the door with Tim, and without making eye contact with my family or Linda, said that we would not be long and would be back in time for supper.

With my heart pounding at a pace a racehorse could only compete with, and my head swimming with unending, unanswered questions just waiting to jump out of my mouth, we set out on our walk. The direction we were walking was of little concern to me as I began grilling Tim with my questions. The more I asked, the more frustrated I became, especially at the calm disposition Tim displayed amid my fear, anxiousness, and uncertainty. "How can he be so calm while I am so in knots? What makes this guy different?" I thought.

Being considerably late, Tim and I were gone for about two hours. Linda and my two-year-old daughter Emilie went for a drive to find us (unbeknownst to me)—we (at least myself) had lost all track of time. I was later told that Linda and Emilie had seen Tim and me walking up a hill

Searching

toward their vehicle without us seeing them. Rather than interrupting us, they just watched us from the vehicle. Linda turned to Emilie and asked, "Do you think Tim will be a good friend for your daddy?" Emilie replied, "Yes, because now my daddy won't cry anymore." From the mouth of babes, my two-year-old daughter spoke prophetic words that were about to come to life in ways I would never have imagined.

Tim and I finally arrived back home. Linda and Deb were very gracious in light of us being late, and we settled down to supper. Our dining table was nestled in the kitchen area which had a doorway leading to a carpeted sitting room, another doorway leading to the hallway, and another door leading out onto the back deck. There were eight of us all together, so there was lots of room. We had a nice visit around the table as we ate, but before long, the clock struck 8:00 p.m. and it was time to tuck the kids in for bed. After the usual bedtime routine, the kids were settled in their rooms, and Deb and I returned to the kitchen table where we began our Bible study, led by Tim, on the book of Revelation.

All I remember about the study was I was still under the grip of fear, anxiety, and uncertainty, and that I asked unending questions to which Tim calmly responded. The uninterrupted study went on from about 8:00 p.m. to 4:30 a.m. at which time Tim, who was sitting to my left, turned to me, looked directly at me, and said, "I will send you no more burdens." It was Tim's mouth and voice through which those words came, but they were not Tim's words. It was not possible that Tim was the one allowing these struggles I had been experiencing over the last week. He said, "*I* will send you no more burdens." That "*I*," I believe, was God, and through His Holy Spirit, He was speaking to me through Tim; I just knew it! I immediately got up out of my chair, walked into the adjacent sitting room, looked up to the ceiling as to Heaven, and finally realized what it meant to give my heart to Jesus. Though I do not remember any specific words I said, if any, I do know that in my heart, I called out to Him to save me from my sin and surrendered myself, my plans, my desires, my goals, my failures, and my fears to Him that I might live for Him and not myself. I finally realized that giving my heart to Jesus meant placing my faith in Him and giving my whole self to Him.

I do not know how long I stood in the sitting room, but I remember the change that came over me—and it was real! As I stood there, I also heard the Lord speak to me, through the Holy Spirit, and say, "You do not have to go through the Tribulation, because I am coming back to get you" (reflective of John 14:1-3). My fears were finally relieved. I had turned to the One who knew. I knew now, that as a true believer, Jesus was coming back to rescue His people (true believers) before the Tribulation—a fact, after considering differing views on this topic, that has been further solidified by my own intense study of this topic.

When I returned to the dining table, before I even said a word, they could see that change had taken place. I was different, and it could be seen in my demeanor. They could see that God had transformed and changed me—I was a new creation in Christ (2 Corinthians 5:17). My fear, anxiety, and uncertainty were changed to joy, peace, and excitement. It felt like a giant needle full of adrenaline had been shot into my veins and I was pumped!

Searching

As we chatted, or as I chatted, around the table about what had transpired, my attention was drawn to something toward the ceiling above the table where we were sitting. As I looked, I could clearly see an eagle's wing, one that was as real as you or I, the detail of which was unmistakable. It seemed to cover the table as if protecting us (Psalm 91:4). I looked back at everyone else and said, "Do you see that?" No one else did; I looked back, and it was gone, but they genuinely believed me that it had been there. Though I did not understand the implication of that vision, I later realized God was showing me that His hand was watching over me and those around the table (as He does all true believers). I can still see that wing in my mind today.

It was close to 5:00 or 5:30 a.m. before any of us got to bed, but I could not sleep. As a result, I was up at around 6:30 a.m. cooking breakfast for everyone, as Tim and Linda needed to get going on their way that morning. After they left, I was excited and driven to share what had happened with my parents. I remember standing by the phone, which was attached to the kitchen wall, and I was facing into the hallway. As I was holding the phone, everything around me disappeared and all that was left was white. Nothing else could be seen. I then saw two large, red-covered books; the one on the left was open and the one to the right was closed. Two large hands appeared. The hands closed the book on the left and opened the book on the right. With a white-feathered quill pen, the right hand wrote my name in this book, and then the vision disappeared. I realized later, I believe, that God was showing me that my name had now been entered into the Book of Life (Revelation 21:22-27; Philippians 4:3).

After that vision disappeared, I got Mom and Dad on the phone to share with them what had happened in the early morning hours that day. Mom and Dad were very gracious as I shared with them what had been happening in my life, but it was foreign to them. So much so, that Mom and Dad came to visit sometime later, out of concern for me, thinking I was having an emotional breakdown or something. Dad, while Mom stayed with Deb and the kids, took me away for the weekend to see if that would straighten me out. Their intentions were caring and honourable, but it became apparent to them that I was serious about the change that had come about through faith in Christ, and that this was not some emotional reaction to something. Though they did not understand, they respected my position.

That same week, our friend Linda encouraged a student of Deb's, whose family we had become friends with, to call me to talk about what had happened to me. As I spoke to her on the phone, I could sense that she was skeptical and wary of what I was sharing with her; her responses seemed to convey that I was a bit off my rocker, but that did not deter me. Our conversation ended amicably, and I thanked her for calling after which I started to climb our staircase and broke down crying. It was a deep, anguished cry. God seemed to be showing me the pain and sadness He feels when one rejects Him, just as this student seemed to have. It was an insight into God's love for mankind and His yearning desire for them to come to the knowledge of the Truth and be saved (1 Timothy 2:4; Luke 19:10).

My prayer was that, if I had the opportunity to share my faith with someone else, God would allow it to be in a

Searching

one-on-one situation. One day while at home, I sensed God prompting me to walk down to the local gas station owned and operated by a fellow named Gary Ford, and witness to him. I headed out the front door and walked to the station, hoping that I could talk with him one-on-one. I remember thinking to myself that I would not share my faith with him unless it was indeed one-on-one. When I arrived at the station, I sat down in the waiting area; Gary was seated at his desk. Gary and I had struck up a friendship over the past year or so, so I was quite comfortable just dropping in on him. There was a problem though, at least in my mind. As I was about to enter into a conversation about my faith, a police cruiser pulled up for gas. The officer then came into the station, and one of the mechanics from the service bay poked his head in, where Gary and I were, and the three of them struck up a conversation with each other. I thought my opportunity was gone.

I remember getting up out of my chair to look out the window and I heard the whisper, "Trust Me" (John 14:1). No sooner did I hear those words, the police officer and the mechanic left. My opportunity had come, and Gary and I had a great conversation. He was not put off in any way but was genuinely interested in what I had to say. We finished our conversation with small talk and then I headed home; I wonder what impact that meeting had on Gary's life.

When I got home, I began to tear up out of joy that I was able to share my faith and that God had honoured my desire to do that one-on-one. It was also a lesson that God is more than capable to set the stage for the sharing of one's faith.

After turning into bed one evening, I had a dream. In that dream, I saw my right arm. My arm looked like it had been burned and charred, but underneath was a new, completely healthy arm. I realized, upon waking up, I believe I was being shown I was a new creation; the old was gone and the new had come (2 Corinthians 5:17). On another occasion, as I laid in bed, the following words came into my mind, "Do not let anyone steal the crown that you have now been given" (Revelation 3:11). I believe God was assuring me and affirming to me that I was indeed His child, that I was saved from the consequences of my sin, and that I was now His.

Up to this point I had been involved with martial arts for several years, both Karate and Tae Kwon Do. I enjoyed it, participated with some men from our church in it, and did well at it, though I was no Bruce Lee (a martial arts icon) by any stretch of the imagination. I spent much time before those early morning events I had just walked through, training and practicing in this art, so much so, that at times it occupied a good portion of my time and mind. I remember standing at the sink one day doing dishes, a day or two after becoming a Christian. As I stood there, the thought came to mind, "Did I trust martial arts more than God to be my protector?" It was not that martial arts were bad, or that involvement in it was wrong if the spiritual aspect of it is omitted. I believe God was showing me that I was looking more to martial arts than God as my and my family's protector. I had become self-reliant rather than reliant on God through my involvement; my mindset was wrong. God, I realized, was calling me to make a decision. A decision to place my trust in Him to look after me and my family—our safety, our needs, etc.—or to place that trust in martial arts. I chose to terminate my martial arts membership and place my trust in the Lord.

This decision did not sit very well with one other person at our church who I had been training with. His name was André, and he was baffled as to why I came to the decision I had. He was so baffled that he approached me after church one Sunday wanting to talk about it, which led to him coming to our house, a day or two later, to continue our conversation. I explained to him my reasoning and why it was the right decision for me, but he found it hard to accept. Sadly, our relationship became distant as a result. I think he may have felt that I abandoned our friendship somehow by opting out of an activity we both had enjoyed.

It was still August and returning to the classroom was just over the horizon, but my priorities had now changed. My desire was not to return to the public school classroom. All I wanted to do now was pack my bags and head to the mission field, but God had other plans (Proverbs 16:9; 19:21). Little did I know that those plans would, in two years, lead us back to Saskatchewan, the place to which I had not long ago said I would like to return. My, and my family's, journey had just begun.

Epilogue

This short book is my personal story of how I came to a saving knowledge of Jesus Christ. Saving knowledge, because I realized that I was a sinner and needed Christ's forgiveness to save me from the consequences of that sin (Romans 6:23). It is a story of how God desires to draw people to Himself and, in doing so, continually pursues them, for He *wants all men to be saved and come to a knowledge of the truth* (1 Timothy 2:4). It is a story of how God, in His desire to draw me to the Truth, planted seeds in my life over time to get my attention that would eventually take root and lead me to genuine faith in Him. It is also the story of how I came to realize that becoming a Christian had nothing to do with religion, accepting a set of rules and regulations, or adhering to some ritual. No! Becoming a Christian had everything to do with relationship—a personal relationship with a real Person, in the Person of Jesus Christ, God's Son.

Becoming a believer also meant, that although sin and Satan had dominion and control over me before salvation (Romans 6:20-21; Romans 6:16), I was now set free from their bondage (Romans 6:18; John 8:32; Acts 10:38). I was now, not a sinner in God's eyes, but a saint (Romans 1:7; 8:27; Ephesians 1:18; 6:18), because of my faith in what Christ did for me on the cross. This does not mean however, that I or other believers do not sin, make wrong choices, or make mistakes (Romans 7:21-25), but because I have now been given the Holy Spirit to reside within me (2 Corinthians 1:21-22) I have the power to resist Satan's temptations and choose not to sin (James 4:7; 1 Peter 5:8-9). That was not the case before my conversion.

Being viewed as a saint by God also does not mean that one is perfect. I, as well as my fellow believers, am on a journey of sanctification (1 Thessalonians 5:23-24), being molded by God into the likeness of His Son, step by step. It is a process and it takes time, but God has promised, as He has to all true believers, He will bring the work He began in me, and all believers, to completion until that day I finally get to see Jesus face-to-face (Philippians 1:6).

As for the paradoxical question I grappled with, namely, "Should not what we believe in (faith) impact who we are in private and public life?" I came to realize, after becoming a Christian, some important learning regarding this issue. The apostle Paul urges us, as believers, *to live a life worthy of the calling you have received* (Ephesians 4:1). He goes on to say, *whatever happens, conduct yourselves in a manner worthy of the gospel of Christ* (Philippians 1:27), and in Colossians 1:10: *we pray this in order that you may live a life worthy of the Lord and may please Him in every way: bearing fruit in every good work, growing in*

Epilogue

the knowledge of God. There is no question that there is the expectation that the believer is to strive to live a life that is pleasing to God—in all circumstances and in all settings. This, however, is not done in our own strength, as that would be impossible. It is accomplished with the power of God through His Holy Spirit. Paul says, **His** *divine power has given us everything we need for life and godliness through our knowledge of him who called us by his own glory and goodness* (2 Peter 1:3, emphasis mine).

As a believer that is my goal, but because growing into the likeness of Christ is a process, there will be times I will fail. The wonderful truth is that when I do, *if we confess our sins, he is faithful and just and will forgive us our sins and purify us from all unrighteousness* (1 John 1:9). I do not have to grovel in that failure! God forgives me, dusts me off, and encourages me to move forward in His strength. Knowing that it is God that works within me to bring about the changes that He desires for me, and that it is a process—a process in which I know there will be times I will trip and fall, God says in Hebrews 12:1, *Therefore, since we are surrounded by such a great cloud of witnesses, let us throw off everything that hinders and the sin that so easily entangles, and let us run with* **perseverance** *the race marked out for us* (emphasis mine). Do not let failure stop you from living for Christ—keep running the race!

Reflecting on this caused me to realize that the fellow who had attended the Antioch II retreat, who gave me a look as though he would bite my head off if he had the opportunity, may have genuinely had a bad day. I realize now that his response to me was not a sure-fire indicator as to whether he was a genuine believer, nor was it a sure-fire indicator that he wasn't. He too may have been in process. In other words, a person who portrays himself or herself as living a clean and moral life is not a reliable indicator that that person is a genuine believer in Christ, just as a person who has the occasional bad day, showing a lapse in graciousness, is not a reliable indicator of unbelief.

Within the first couple of weeks of becoming a believer, our friend Linda came to our house for a visit. During that visit, Linda handed me a poem entitled, "The Last Call." The poem goes as follows:

> Like a fool
> I went away,
> Said, "Later, Lord,
> Another day."
>
> God's Holy Son
> Extended grace
> And whispered, "Child,
> I took your place."
>
> "Lord, I know
> You showed Your love for me
> But there are other things
> I'd rather be."
>
> "When I'm ready
> I'll come. You'll see."
> "My Child," He said,
> "I died for thee."
>
> "Tomorrow, Lord,"
> That's what I said.

Epilogue

"Child," He questioned,
"What lies ahead?"

"Lord, I'll think about
What all You've said.
Maybe You're right.
I don't know what lies ahead."

As He reached out His hand,
I looked into His loving face
And knew I could no longer wait.
Tomorrow might be too late.

"Thank you, Lord," I whispered,
"For caring about me."
"My child," He said,
"I've just been waiting for thee."

With an outstretched hand,
He reached and restored,
Changed my life and made
Me whole.

What glory shone around!
Joy flooded over me.
Tears so filled my eyes
That I could hardly see.

When I looked up,
He was gone.
But I could feel His presence.
His glory lingered on.

He'd simply come
One last time
To see If I would
Change my mind.

Author Unknown

After reading that poem, I had the conviction that God was telling me that had I not responded to Him calling me at that time, I would have continued in my religious moralism and grown in hardness of heart to the point that I would have become numb to God's outstretched hand. I thank God that I responded, that He did not give up on me, and that He gave me another opportunity! In my case, an opportunity that could have been my last.

I was a religious moralist. Religious in that I went to church; read the Bible; prayed; had head knowledge of Jesus, God, and the Holy Spirit; and could easily fit into a church setting. I was a moralist in that I tried to be a good person, do the right things, and do good works. These things were not bad in themselves, but I learned later that attitudes and actions are not necessarily reliable indicators that a person is a genuine follower of Christ. There was a key factor that was missing. That key factor was a personal relationship with Jesus Christ. I had not asked Jesus to forgive me for my sins and accept His free gift of forgiveness and eternal life—not until the early morning hours of August 14, 1992. I was thirty-two years old. For years God had been planting seeds in my life and putting things and people in front of me to get my attention. In my case, the biggest thing God put in front of me to get my attention was the coming Biblical event called the Tribulation. I did not want to be left behind nor does He want you to!

Epilogue

There are many views held by genuine, godly believers concerning the Tribulation and whether true believers will be left on the earth to experience it in whole, in part, or not at all. Sadly, these differing views have led, in some cases, to division and broken fellowship among believers. This topic, along with Bible prophecy, should be engaged with the attitude of Proverbs 27:17: *As iron sharpens iron, so one man sharpens another*. We are meant to look into what God's Word says and study it together to help sharpen one another's understanding of it. It is not meant to be divisive! The scope of this book, however, is not intended for me to fully explain my stance on the Tribulation and the believer's relation to it. Consequently, I have included some reputable resources, in the resource chapter of this book, for your perusal and personal study to come to your own conclusions.

Through the wisdom of more mature believers, long ago I was cautioned to take everything I hear, read, and see (visions and dreams for example), and take them back to Scripture to make sure it lines up with the Word of God. In my experience in the sitting room that early morning back in Grafton, I believe God did say to me that I did not have to go through the Tribulation because He was coming back for me (and all true believers) in an event called the Rapture (1 Thessalonians 4:13-18; 1 Corinthians 15:51-52; Revelation 3:10). It was a lesson in that true believers, of which I had now become, will escape (Luke 21:36) the horrors of the Tribulation; before my conversion I could not claim that promise.

God knows what each person needs to get their attention. Some of the ways God gets people's attention may be similar but not necessarily identical; therefore, it is important to be very cautious about comparing conversion testimonies. In most cases they will be different, with some being less dramatic than others, but no less significant. God knew I needed those visions He gave me of the eagle's wing and the hands with the two books because He knew I would need, later in life, to look back on those events as signposts that I belong to Him. It is important, however, to remember that although God can and does use visions, etc., our assurance needs to come from and be firmly based on God's Word and His promises—not experiences.

SOME QUESTIONS FOR REFLECTION:

1. Where are you in this journey of life? Are you a religious moralist?
2. Do you have faith and, if so, what or who is that faith based in or on?
3. What seeds has God been placing in your life to get your attention? Have you been ignoring them, writing them off as coincidence?
4. Have you been putting off recognizing that you need to make your decision regarding Christ's free gift of forgiveness and eternal life? How many opportunities do you think you will have?
5. Are you saying to God's outstretched hand, "When I'm ready, I'll come?"
6. What if this was your last opportunity to accept God's free gift of salvation? Your next day is not guaranteed.

Epilogue

Jesus said, *I tell you, now is the time of God's favor, now is the day of salvation* (2 Corinthians 6:2) and *Salvation is found in no one else, for there is no other name under heaven given to men by which we must be saved* (Acts 4:12). If you are one who is sitting on the fence regarding whether or not to accept God's free gift of salvation, I want to encourage you to wait no longer. We have no guarantees of tomorrow other than eternity, but where will you spend it? Accepting God's free gift of forgiveness and salvation is as easy as A, B, C:

A—Admit that you are a sinner. This is where godly sorrow leads to genuine repentance or a turning away from sinning against a righteous God. There is a change of heart and a change of mind; God changes our hearts and regenerates us (makes us into a new person) from the inside out (Romans 3:10; 3:23; 6:23; Ephesians 2:8-9).

B—Believe in your heart that Jesus Christ died for your sins, was buried, and that God raised Jesus from the dead. This is trusting with all your heart that Jesus Christ is who He said He was (Romans 10:9-10).

C—Call upon the name of the Lord. This is calling out to God to save you from your sins and to receive His free gift of forgiveness and eternal life (Romans 14:11; 10:13).

My journey began when I received God's free gift of forgiveness and eternal life and I am still on that journey, either until I die or when Jesus comes back to take His Church in the Rapture.

Where are you in your journey?

Examine yourselves to see whether you are in the faith; test yourselves... (2 CORINTHIANS 13:5)

Resources

Crone, Billy. *The Rapture: Don't Be Deceived.* Get A Life Ministries Inc., 2016.

Jeremiah, Dr. David. *Agents of the Apocalypse.* Carol Stream, Illinois: Tyndale House Publishers Inc., 2014.

Markell, Jan. *Are We Living in The Last Days?* Maple Grove, MN: Olive Tree Ministries, 2016.

Rhodes, Ron. *The End Times in Chronological Order.* Eugene, Oregon: Harvest House Publishers, 2012.

LaHaye, Tim, and Ed Hindson. *Exploring Bible Prophecy from Genesis to Revelation.* Eugene, Oregon: Harvest House Publishers, 2006.

Rhodes, Ron. *Jesus and the End Times.* Eugene, Oregon: Harvest House Publishers, 2019.

CPSIA information can be obtained
at www.ICGtesting.com
Printed in the USA
BVHW041804030921
615645BV00006B/11